MW01378204

Do You Know for Sure GOD the Father Has Your Back?

A Grandfather's Journey: Sharing Wisdom and Faith

Reza Mohseni

ISBN 979-8-89243-608-3 (paperback)
ISBN 979-8-89345-018-7 (hardcover)
ISBN 979-8-89243-609-0 (digital)

Copyright © 2024 by Reza Mohseni

All rights reserved. No part of this publication may be reproduced, distributed, or transmitted in any form or by any means, including photocopying, recording, or other electronic or mechanical methods without the prior written permission of the publisher. For permission requests, solicit the publisher via the address below.

Christian Faith Publishing
832 Park Avenue
Meadville, PA 16335
www.christianfaithpublishing.com

Printed in the United States of America

References and Citations

World English Bible (WEB) - The World English Bible is in the Public Domain. That means that it is not copyrighted. However, "World English Bible" is a Trademark.
New Living Translation (NLT) - Scripture quotations marked (NLT) are taken from the Holy Bible, New Living Translation, copyright © 1996, 2004, 2007 by Tyndale House Foundation. Used by permission of Tyndale House Publishers, Inc., Carol Stream, Illinois 60188. All rights reserved.
The Message (MSG) - Scripture taken from The Message. Copyright © 1993, 1994, 1995, 1996, 2000, 2001, 2002. Used by permission of NavPress Publishing Group.
New International Version (NIV) - THE HOLY BIBLE, NEW INTERNATIONAL VERSION®, NIV® Copyright © 1973, 1978, 1984, 2011 by Biblica, Inc.® Used by permission. All rights reserved worldwide.
Amplified Bible (AMP) - Copyright © 2015 by The Lockman Foundation, La Habra, CA 90631. All rights reserved.
King James Bible & NKJV Online (www.kingjamesbibleonline.org) has been online since November 2007 as dedicated King James Bible website. King James Version Bible Ebook in PDF, EPUB, MOBI, or Word file format. Works offline!
GotQuestion.org
Bible Study Tools
BBN Global
Crosswalk.com
Christianity.com

Biblegateway.com
Knowing-jesus.com
1999 Father Heart Communications - FathersLoveLetter.com
gotquestions.org- Copyright 2002-2023 Got Questions Ministries.
All rights reserved. This page last updated: January 4, 2022
"The Ten Commandments" – By Dennis Prager
I must tell Jesus all my trials Author: E. A. Hoffman (1894)
"What do I want for my Childrens"- Author:
Ruth Anderson and Bette Sloat
"O be careful little eyes what you see"- Copy right
1956 by Zondervan Music Publishers
"Amazing Grace." It was written by Chris
Tomlin, Louie Giglio, and John Newton.
"I have decided to follow Jesus" by songwriters: Leslie B. Tucker

Dedication

This book is dedicated with heartfelt gratitude and love to those who have made my life a remarkable journey.

First and foremost, to my beloved wife, Faezeh, my confidant, my love, and my unwavering supporter, who has walked every step of this incredible journey by my side.

To my dear children and their loving spouses—Sean and Lauren, Rachel and Richard, Yasi and Eman, Michelle and Jonathan, and Casey. You have taught me more about life and love than I could have ever collected from a thousand books.

To my ten cherished grandchildren—Ethan, Ellie, Gabe, Madi, Nolan, Clara, Richy, Mila, Ruby, and to the little one who is soon to join our family in April 2024. My love for each of you grows with every passing day.

I want to say a heartfelt thank you to my family for always supporting and loving me. Your encouragement has given me strength, and I am forever grateful.

I am also indebted to the countless individuals who have crossed my path on this spiritual journey. Your wisdom, encouragement, and shared experiences have shaped the words on these pages. With heartfelt gratitude, I extend my warmest thanks to both my cherished friends and those I have yet to meet. To each of you reading this, I wholeheartedly hope that the unfolding pages bring you inspiration and profound reassurance. Your presence in this journey means more to me than words can express.

Above all, my gratitude knows no bounds when I think of the One who has been my constant guide, my unyielding support, and my unfailing love. To God the Father, the Son, and the Holy Spirit, who indeed has had my back, my heart sings with praise. In moments of joy, in times of struggle, and throughout the winding roads of life, I have felt His presence, His guidance, His grace, and His unending love.

I pray that as you begin on this journey through the words of this book, you too will come to know the depth of His love, the certainty of His guidance, and the assurance that, indeed, God the Father has your back.

With profound gratitude and unwavering faith and with deep appreciation!

Contents

Introduction

In Gratitude for His Unfailing Love

As I write this, I am really thankful for the journey of faith that brought me here. *Do You Know for Sure if God the Father Has Your Back* isn't just a book to me; it's about how God's love shaped my life.

Looking back, I see God's constant presence and kindness. This book is like a labor of love, born from prayer, both in good and tough times, and from knowing a caring and forgiving God.

In a world where things can be confusing, it's our job as a child of God to help everyone—our kids, families, friends, and our communities— to understand what truly matters. The Bible tells us to study and know the truth well (2 Timothy 2:15). It's about not just knowing the truth but also comprehending it deeply and accurately.

In a world that's confusing and uncertain, knowing what is true helps us tackle life's problems and guide others to understand things better. As someone who believes in God, I really enjoy helping our family, friends, and community see what's important. It can make a big difference and give us a clear sense of purpose.

God is the truth. That means He's always fair and always right. He is the Rock. His work is perfect: for all his ways are judgment: a God of truth and without iniquity, just and right is he (Deuteronomy 32:4).

Many people say they believe in God, but not everyone feels the amazing peace that comes from giving up control of God and letting

God be in control. I want my family, friends, and everyone I care about to feel safe and confident because of their connection and relationship with God. Understanding that God forgives our mistakes and gives us a fresh start when we follow Him brings a special sense of safety and confidence. It helps us be on the right track when we decide to follow Him.

The most important thing in life is to be close to God and to love Him. Often, we get too busy with our lives and forget to spend time with God. It's crucial to stop and think about what it truly means to seek God.

Today, many things distract us from wholeheartedly seeking God. I believe that after being saved, seeking God becomes the most critical part of being a Christian.

Truly knowing God requires seeking Him with all our heart, just like Jeremiah 29:13 says. However, very few of us have this close relationship because it needs things like humility, setting aside our own wants, praying honestly, and worshiping with all our hearts.

This isn't meant to discourage us but to show us how vital it is to bring our hearts back to God through conviction, a gift from Him.

This book aims to make everyone consider how they're linked to God and their relationship with Him. I want my family and friends to see the good things that happen when we're close to God and the not-so-good things when we're not.

Sometimes, life is easy for some but harder for others. It's important to be patient and help those who are having a tough time. Instead of only thinking about ourselves, we should care about what helps others. Let's team up to make everyone's faith stronger.

I am writing this book for the people I care about—my family and friends—to share important lessons from the Bible. These teachings talk about being truthful, making smart decisions, being kind, leaving behind good things, and guiding based on what the Bible teaches about what's good and how to lead a meaningful and purposeful life.

Biography

My name is Reza Mohseni, and I was born and raised in Tehran, Iran. In my youth, I was highly athletic, and soccer became my favorite sport. In 1977, when I was seventeen years old, my father, Major General Abbas Mohseni, orchestrated a journey for me to the United States. This incredible journey I've been on isn't just a path I've walked; it's a story shaped by the love and kindness of some incredible souls within our family.

I owe an immeasurable debt of gratitude to my late uncle, Dr. Fariborz "Fari" Rahbar, and his wonderful wife, Aunt Carol Ann Rahbar. Their unwavering support and love have been my guiding light, making this journey possible in countless ways. They've stood by me, believing in my dreams and urging me to reach for them.

Then there's my dear cousin, Dr. Amir Rahbar, and his dear wife, Michelle, along with their lovely children, Alexandra and Isabelle.

And not to forget my other cousin, Shalah R Adam, and her dear husband, Lawrence Adam, along with their beautiful children, Yasmine, Aleah, and Arianna.

With over fifty-five years of living experience in the United States, my uncle's family became a guiding light throughout my American journey.

I arrived in the United States in December 1977, leaving my home and loved ones behind. It was a difficult decision, but my parents assured me that they, along with my three brothers, would join me within a couple of years.

Following my father's wishes, I was welcomed by my late Uncle Fari, a distinguished professor of Medicine at Howard University in Washington, DC. He had become a board-certified neonatologist and had served as the director of Newborn Services at Howard University Hospital. I spent my first few months in the United States under my Uncle Fari and Aunt Carol's roof, and with his support and guidance, I secured my first apartment in College Park, Maryland.

I joined Northwestern High School in Hyattsville, Maryland, with the goal of earning my high school diploma. Remarkably, I achieved this milestone in just a few months. My passion for soccer found expression on the school's team, where I led by example and emerged as the top scorer, setting a record with over forty goals for Northwestern High School.

However, as I settled into my new life, an unexpected turn of events occurred in Iran. The Iranian Revolution erupted, an intense and transformative period that led to the fall of the monarchy of Shah Mohammad Reza Pahlavi and the establishment of an Islamic republic under Ayatollah Ruhollah Khomeini. This revolution raged from January 1978 to February 11, 1979, lasting a year, one month, and four days, with the peak of protests and strikes occurring in the fall of 1978.

Due to the ensuing hostage crisis in Iran between 1979 and 1980, my family found themselves unable to leave Iran and join me in the United States. All communication with Iran was severed. As a result, my parents were no longer able to provide support, leaving me alone in a foreign country at the tender age of eighteen.

Undeterred, I pressed on with my educational journey and enrolled at Prince George's Community College (PGCC). My love for soccer led me to lead the college's soccer team, to which I contributed by scoring twenty-six goals during the season. It was my passion for the sport that opened doors for me, and I was eventually awarded a full soccer scholarship from the University of Maryland. This scholarship covered all my living and college expenses.

At the University of Maryland, I continued to shine in the realm of soccer, becoming the goals and points leader in 1982. My journey in the United States was marked by challenges, but it also paved the way for incredible achievements and opportunities that shaped my life and experiences.

My Testimony

I want to take this opportunity to share with you how God transformed my life and how I was "born again" through my journey of faith.

The journey started in 1978 when I was a high school student at Northwestern High School in the United States. It was during that time that I met my only American Christian girlfriend, Terri Tipton, whom I loved dearly, and we married in 1981. We have four beautiful, amazing children for whom I am forever blessed.

Unfortunately, Terri passed away and never got the opportunity to get to know our many beautiful grandchildren, but she will forever hold a special place in all our hearts. Because of my marriage to Terri, I was truly blessed.

Terri's dear mom, Gayle, and her dad, Robert Tipton, hold a special place in my heart. Terri's mom later married Ronald Hamilton (fondly known as "Pop"), and he adored and doted on her and our children like they were his own. Pop is very dear to me and the whole family.

Terri's cherished sister, Anngi, is especially dear to me. Pop's son, dear Ronnie, is married to dear Gayla, and they have an incredible son named Kenny, who recently married Caitlin.

In our extended family, we remember Terri's late grandmother, Elizabeth (known as "Mother" to her children and grandchildren alike), and her late grandfather, Herbert Nelson, known as Pappaw. They were blessed with four children: Patricia (Pat), Herbert, Gayle, and Sue.

Terri's oldest aunt, the late Aunt Pat, was married to Norman, and they had three daughters. Their eldest daughter, dear Lesli, is married to dear Andy. Lesli and Andy are blessed with four wonderful children: Stacie, Emily, Katie, and Julie. Aunt Pat's middle daughter, dear Nanci, was married to Allen, and they have four lovely children: Jonathan, Jared, Lydia, and Sophie. The youngest daughter of Aunt Pat, the late dear Kelli, died suddenly at eighteen years old, and she holds a special place in all our hearts.

Terri's Uncle Herbert married Cindy, and they had three beautiful children named Denielle, Katrina, and Meghan, who were all married. Denielle has two adorable boys (Case and Colton), and Meghan has two adorable girls (Elsie and Rory).

Terri has another dear aunt named Sue, who was married to the late Steven Kochel, known as Uncle Steve. Their firstborn, Brent, is married to Tammy, and they have two adorable children, Brooke and Morgan (from Tammy's first marriage). Aunt Sue's middle son, Jason, is married to Desiree, and they have three adorable children, Peyton, Finn, and Piper. Aunt Sue's youngest son, the late Joshua, was married to Aida, and they have two beautiful children named Stevie and Abbie Sue.

Through my marriage to Terri, I was introduced to Christianity. Terri, Mother, Aunt Pat, Lesli, and Andy played significant roles in sharing the faith with me.

Aunt Pat gifted me my first Persian Bible. When I read it in Farsi, it deeply moved me, bringing tears to my eyes and filling my heart with immense joy.

Terri was unlike anyone I had ever known. Her joy, truthfulness, modesty, and kindness touched my heart in a profound way. She had qualities that I longed for but knew I lacked. Her character and her relationship with God were remarkable. Her influence on me was undeniable.

When our first child was born, Terri insisted that our son, Sean, attend a Christian school, which he did. Sean started learning about Jesus at Temple Baptist School (TBS); and eventually, with his mother's guidance, he came to believe in Jesus Christ even before I did.

I remember how Sean would eagerly invite me to join him for church every Sunday, and I eventually accepted his invitations. My first experience with church was at Temple Baptist Church (TBC), where Pastor David Pitman passionately preached the message of Jesus Christ. The congregation at TBC was warm and welcoming, and I felt embraced by the church community.

During one particular service, I vividly remember the choir singing the hymn "Victory in Jesus" by Eugene Monroe Bartlett, and The Holy Spirit of God deeply touched my heart. The lyrics resonated with me so much that I like to pen it here:

> I heard an old, old story how a Savior came from glory, How He gave His life on Calvary to save a wretch like me; I heard about His groaning, of His precious blood's atoning,
>
> Then I repented of my sins and won the victory.
>
> O victory in Jesus, my Savior, forever. He sought me and bought me with His redeeming blood; He loved me ere I knew Him, and all my love is due Him, He plunged me to victory beneath the cleansing flood.
>
> I heard about His healing, of His cleansing power revealing. How He made the lame to walk again and caused the blind to see; And then I cried, "Dear Jesus, come and heal my broken spirit," And somehow Jesus came and brought to me the victory. O victory in Jesus, my Savior, forever. He sought me and bought me with His redeeming blood; He loved me ere I knew Him, and all my love is due Him, He plunged me to victory beneath the cleansing flood.
>
> I heard about a mansion He has built for me in glory. And I heard about the streets of gold beyond the crystal sea; About the angels singing

> and the old redemption story, And some sweet day I'll sing up there the song of victory.
>
> O victory in Jesus, my Savior, forever. He sought me and bought me with His redeeming blood; He loved me ere I knew Him, and all my love is due Him, He plunged me to victory beneath the cleansing flood.

Now I want to share with you the story of my spiritual journey, which began with a pivotal moment in my life.

A few months passed, and my son's great-grandmother, affectionately known as Mother, became seriously ill. As her condition worsened, she expressed a heartfelt desire for me to visit her at the hospital. During our visit, as Mother held my hand, she revealed something that touched me profoundly. She said, "Dear Reza, I want you to know that I've been praying for you, and I know the Lord wants you to get saved because He loves you more than anyone has ever loved you before." Her words had a profound impact on my heart.

Following Mother's passing, our family was invited to her "homegoing" celebration at our church. The concept of a homegoing ceremony was entirely foreign to me, and it left me questioning its meaning. I couldn't understand how a deceased person could be going home. During the ceremony at Temple Baptist Church (TBC), I had the opportunity to hear the gospel once again from Pastor Pitman. What struck me was the immense joy in everyone's hearts, which was truly astonishing. Witnessing people rejoicing at a funeral stirred a deep curiosity within me about how I could be certain of my own path to heaven.

Pastor Pitman delivered the gospel message, explaining that Mother had been saved and had placed her trust in Jesus alone during her life. Now after her passing, she was going home to be with Jesus in heaven forever. This prompted me to pray during the funeral. "Dear God, forgive me of my sins and thank you for opening my understanding so I can know and trust Jesus as the way, the truth, and the life" (John 14:6). I stepped forward to Pastor Pitman and accepted Christ that day at the cemetery, and this marked a transformative moment in my life. The funeral was filled with a remarkable sense of joy.

After this significant event, I'd like to share how my relationship with the Lord Jesus has grown, and how He has become my dearest friend.

Following my salvation, I eagerly awaited miraculous changes in my life. Instead, I felt a deep desire within me to read and write the entire New Testament word by word, driven by a longing to meet the Lord of the Bible. This desire was so intense that it kept me awake for many nights, captivated by the Scriptures. Reading His words brought peace to my soul, and I realized that my soul thirsted for Him, and no one else could quench that thirst.

I began to feel my Lord in my heart. Imagine a man who has lived his whole life in the desert and who has never seen the ocean in his life, finding himself on the beach standing in front of the ocean.

He is excited yet marveling because he sees no end to it. A special moment of great joy takes over his soul. Out of exceeding joy, he runs toward the ocean, reaches down, and grabs some water in his hand.

Feeling the thrill of having found the ocean, he rejoices in his heart. That's exactly how I felt when I got saved, but soon after, I began to realize how great and deep is this ocean!

I said in my heart, O God, help me. Allow me to come to know you.

Help me, O Lord, reveal yourself to me in the Bible.

Then I began diligently with great love, reading the Bible, looking for my Savior, in search and hope of meeting the Lord.

It was the gospel of John where, for the first time, I felt my Savior talking to me personally. He said, "I am the light of the world: he that followeth me shall not walk in darkness, but shall have the light of life" (John 8:12).

It touched my heart because I knew that where there is darkness, there is also fear. Knowing that my Savior is the light of the world calmed and comforted my heart.

Then I continued my reading till I came to another verse where the Lord says: "I am the bread of life, he that cometh to me shall never hunger, and he that believeth on me shall never thirst" (John 6:35).

Then the Lord said: "But whosoever drinketh of the water that I shall give him, shall never thirst, but the water that I shall give him shall be in him a well of water springing up into everlasting life" (John 4:14).

I said, O God, I want to have this bread and this water.

I knew in my past life that there was nothing that could satisfy my selfish greed and desires. I said in my heart, O God, how can I drink this water?

Then the Lord said: "If any man thirst, let him come unto me, and drink" (John 7:37). And I said, "Lord, I come. I come."

Then the Lord said: "I am the way, the truth, and the life, no man can come unto the father, but by me" (John 14:6). I said in my heart, amen.

You see, I know in my heart that the truth of Jesus Christ had set me free because I had peace and joy in my heart because I know my Savior, and I know my sins are forgiven, and I know I am saved and I have eternal life.

The more I came to know the Lord, the more understanding the Lord gave me. Then I began to understand why the Bible says: Thy word is a lamp unto my feet, and a light unto my path (Psalm 119:105).

By then, I was convinced that the Lord was talking to me personally, and He had clear moral directions for me: directing and preparing my heart for his purpose and will in my life.

Then I noticed that the Lord Jesus says: "The Lord our God is one Lord, and thou shalt love the Lord thy God with all thy heart, and with all thy soul, and with all thy mind, and with all thy strength" (Mark 12:29–30).

You see, the Creator is telling us in many ways throughout the Bible that He knows our hearts. He created us. He knows after Adam sinned, all men fell, and sin entered the world.

He is telling us not to trust our minds because they change. Our minds can be deceitful.

The Bible teaches: "Trust in the Lord with all thine heart: and lean not unto thine own understanding. In all thy ways acknowledge Him, and He shall direct thy paths" (Proverbs 3:5–6).

> Delight thyself also in the Lord, and He shall give thee the desires of thine heart. Commit thy way unto the Lord, and trust also in Him, and He shall bring it to pass. (Psalm 37:3–5)

> You see, God wants us to know that when He created man He did not create a deceitful heart for man: rather, mankind was created in His image. (Genesis 1:26)

God Almighty warned Adam and Eve (before they chose to sin against Him) that if they ate from the Tree of Life, they would die (Genesis 2:16–17).

When Adam and Eve deliberately sinned against God, sin entered into the world. Sin has separated man from his Creator ever since.

That's why God sees sin in us and says not to trust our minds because of our sins. Sin is a destroyer. The Bible teaches: The whole head is sick, and the whole heart faint.

> From the sole of the foot even unto the head there is no soundness in it but wounds and bruises and putrefying sores. (Isaiah 1:5–6)

You see, the Bible says: "If we say that we have no sin we deceive ourselves, and the truth is not in us... If we say that we have not sinned, we make Him a liar, and His word is not in us" (1 John 1:8–10).

The Bible teaches: "He that trusteth in his own heart is a fool" (Proverbs 14:12).

I felt in my heart that the Lord had proven to my soul that His Word is the truth.

In the same way that God warned and commanded Adam and Eve not to eat from the Tree of Life, now the Lord is telling us not to trust our own hearts but rather trust in Him with all of our heart, soul, mind, and strength (Mark 12:29–30).

Do not be afraid of God! Do not be afraid of the truth about ourselves! Do not be afraid of man's weaknesses; come back to God with no fear.

You see, God longs for you. He wants to be your best friend. He wants to bless you, help make those difficult decisions for you, and take over all your burdens and troubles.

He wants to heal your hurts. He wants to give you strength. He wants to make sure you have joy and peace in your heart forever. He wants you to know He loves you and wants to take care of you and your family.

He wants to give you life more abundantly. He is a great and awesome God!

I gave my heart to the Lord Jesus: after all, it's His. Will you do the same? The Bible says: "He is faithful and just to forgive us our sins, and to cleanse us from all unrighteousness" (1 John 1:7). "For God hath not appointed us to wrath, but to obtain salvation by our Lord Jesus Christ" (1 Thessalonians 5:9).

> Believe in the Lord Jesus Christ, and thou shalt be saved. (Acts 16:31)

To My Beloved Family and Adult Children

Writing to my beloved family and adult children aligns with biblical principles for several reasons:

Communication and connection. The Bible emphasizes the importance of communication within families. Writing allows me for continued connection and sharing of thoughts, feelings, and wisdom across distances and time (Proverbs 15:23; Ephesians 4:29).

Passing down wisdom. The Bible encourages passing down wisdom and teachings to the next generations (Proverbs 13:1; Proverbs 22:6). In this book, I share meaningful wisdom, guidance, and important life lessons for my beloved family, friends, and others, aiming to nurture their growth and deepen their understanding.

Expressing love and encouragement. Biblical teachings emphasize love within families and the importance of encouragement (Colossians 3:21; 1 Thessalonians 5:11). Writing this book expresses my love, care, and support, offering encouragement and guidance as they navigate life's challenges.

Forgiveness and reconciliation. The Bible underscores the significance of forgiveness and reconciliation within families (Ephesians 4:32). Writing this book can serve as a means to extend forgiveness, heal past wounds, and foster reconciliation within my family relationships.

Legacy and testament. Sharing my thoughts with our family through writing this book is a way to leave a lasting legacy of our beliefs, values, and experiences. It's a gift of faith, love, and wisdom for both present and future generations to treasure and learn from.

Spiritual guidance. Similar to how biblical figures, like Paul in the New Testament, offered guidance through their letters, my written words in this book can also provide spiritual guidance and encouragement to our family members.

To My Dearest Family

Expressing how much each of you means to me is a challenging task; the memories we've shared over the years often flood my thoughts, reminding me of the countless wonderful moments we've cherished together.

I want to express my deepest gratitude and appreciation for allowing me to build a loving family. Choosing to stay in the same area and be close during our gatherings has made our family exceptionally special and incomparable. I'm sincerely thankful from the depths of my heart. Thank you from the bottom of my heart.

Ever since Jesus entered my life and heart, my ongoing prayer has been for a revival in our home. It brings warmth to my heart that we've stayed together. Whether you choose to stay close or move, I am so glad you have chosen closeness for God's blessings on our family and kids. Our monthly family get-togethers, celebrations, vacations, and holidays are blessings, and God is good.

Understanding life according to the Bible is important for parents. It is like a law of nature; if God is not present, sadly, the devil might be. As God's child, I have learned that getting closer to God keeps the enemy away from our home.

In 2 Chronicles 7:14, it says that if a family is humble and calls to God, He will heal that home.

Dear family, in a family that follows God, everyone plays a role and should remember certain things—seeking God, speaking truthfully, having unconditional love, staying humble, unity, forgiving and serving.

Seeking God. Strengthen family bonds and please God by praying together (Matthew 6:33–34, Hebrews 11:6).

Speaking truth. Show leadership by speaking truth; honesty sets a good example (Proverbs 27:5).

Unconditional love. Love your children equally and raise them with love (1 Corinthians 16:14).

Staying humble. Parents should be humble as children imitate their behavior (James 4:6).

Unity. Unity is crucial; division leads to separation (1 Corinthians 1:10).

Forgiveness. Essential for a Godly family, as advised in Luke 17:3–4 and Mark 11:25.

Serving. Parents should lead by example, showing love and dedication to God (John 12:25-26).

My prayer has always been for unity in our family and protection from the enemy in our home.

As your parent or bubba and as your friend and supporter, nothing has brought me greater joy than witnessing the incredible adults you've grown into. Your journey to this point has been a source of immense pride for me. I'm so incredibly proud of the paths you've chosen and the exceptional individuals you've become.

Life's trials have not deterred you; instead, you've faced them head-on with unwavering courage and determination, achieving remarkable feats. Your strength and perseverance continue to inspire me, and I have no doubt that each of you will achieve even greater things in the future.

I want you to know that my pride in each of you extends far beyond your accomplishments. It's rooted in the incredible people you are—the love and care you show each other, your sensitivity to those around you, and the deep compassion and passion you hold for our family.

My love for you is a steadfast and unwavering force in my life. No matter where life takes you or what challenges you face, remember that my love and support for you are boundless and unconditional.

The memories we've created together are treasures I hold dear, and I eagerly anticipate making many more in the years ahead. Your happiness and well-being will forever be my top priority, and I'll stand by your side, no matter the circumstances.

If ever you need guidance, a listening ear, or a comforting presence, know that you can always turn to me. I'm here to offer my wisdom, share in your joys, and help you navigate life's challenges.

As you continue on your life's journey, I have a few simple wishes for each of you. May you continue to dream big, seize opportunities, and find fulfillment in all your pursuits. Cherish the love and support of family and friends, and let your kindness and light illuminate the world.

Above all, pursue God, love Him, and seek His presence every day. His teachings and wisdom will be your compass throughout life. Embrace the love of our family and shine brightly in the world while finding contentment in your faith and values.

Always remember that God loves you, and His presence will forever be your source of strength and guidance.

To my Dear Wife, Faezeh

I find myself in awe of the incredible strength and unwavering love you've shown throughout our journey together. Your resilience in the face of challenges, your wisdom, and your unwavering support have been my guiding light through every twist and turn. Words can hardly capture the depth of my gratitude.

Your steadfastness in the face of uncertainty and your unyielding spirit in times of difficulty reassure me that you're there for me and our family. Your commitment to fairness and doing what's right continues to inspire me every single day.

Thank you doesn't seem enough for the hard work you put in, not only to keep our family united but also for excelling at your job. Your warmth when I come home, your grace in handling family matters, your delicious cooking, and the unshakeable support you provide mean the world to me, more than words can ever express.

Having you by my side has shaped me into a better person. Your friendship and love have been a guiding light through every step of our journey together, and I'm endlessly grateful for it. My heart swells with love for you.

Reflecting to our wedding day always fills me with the most special memories. Our marriage has given us so much joy, especially welcoming your amazing daughter Yasmin, whom I adore dearly, into our lives. Moreover, having your beloved father, Ali, and your wonderful mother, Foozieh, alongside your dear sister Forough and her dear husband, Mohammad, their awesome son Nima, and also your dear younger brother Reza and his lovely wife, Maral, in our lives has been such a blessing.

Your happiness means the world to me, and I pray for that every day. I would move mountains to see that smile on your face. You've brought so much vibrancy and happiness into my life, and I can't thank you enough for it.

Thank you for being the voice of reason and for finding that middle ground for us. I am incredibly blessed to have such a loyal and loving woman as my wife. Your maturity, intelligence, and your deep connection with the Lord fill my heart with immense love and pride.

With all my love, now and forever.

To My Dear Sean

I just wanted to tell you how happy and proud I am of the amazing person you've become.

Since the day you were born, it's been so wonderful watching you grow up. You were always a special kid, standing out with your caring and loving nature. You were a great listener and had a kind heart, making you truly special.

What makes me really proud is that you've always been good to yourself and others. You've shown kindness as a person, a son, a brother, and a student. I am also very proud of your athleticism! Your skills in soccer and basketball were impressive. I remember how we used to play soccer together during family vacations on the beaches and spare time, and those moments were so much fun. I miss those days, and I'm grateful that we still play soccer together in adulthood. I really cherish these times. But what I love the most is your heart for the Lord. It brings me so much joy to see you love Him and live for Him wholeheartedly.

We've had many great times together, and I miss those moments, especially the "Mohseni's Sandwich" times when all six of us squeezed onto each other. I also have clear memories of how much you loved watching He Man. Every opportunity we had, we would act out those scenes together, and those moments are precious to me.

One of the best moments was witnessing your graduation from Crown College, majoring in pastoral ministries. It made me incredibly proud to see all that you've achieved.

Your wedding day was such a happy time! When I saw you, Lauren, and the arrival of Ethan boy, Ellie Joon, and Nolan boy, it brought a lot of joy to my life. Because of your marriage, our family has been blessed to have Lauren's dear mom, Sherri, and her dear dad, David, and Lauren's dear brother Sean and his wife Amy, and their two adorable kids, Charolette and Savanna. Also, Lauren's younger dear brother Phillip and her younger dear sister Sarah have added warmth to our family.

You are an incredible dad. Your love and dedication to spending time with your kids, teaching them the love of God, and showering them with affection is truly remarkable. It is evident how much joy and fulfillment you find in being with your children, and that brings happiness to me as well.

Years went by along with countless birthdays and Christmas, and *I always thank God for giving me such an understanding and supporting angle like you; you never threw tantrums and always supported me during hard times. Sometimes, you even stepped up and took responsibility for your sisters. Thank you for being such a perfect son.*

Sean, you've grown into an amazing man, and I'm lucky to be your dad. I just wanted to take a moment to remind you of the joy and pride you've given me. Your achievements, your family, and the wonderful person you are today show what incredible character you have. I feel so blessed to be part of your life and amazed that I get to watch you grow and change.

Above all, my dear Sean and Lauren, my most important wish for both of you is to keep building a warm and nurturing home together, as it is the essence of a fulfilling life. Embrace the love that follows the path of Christ; treat each other with kindness and respect, regardless of life's challenges. Build trust and remain loyal. But above all, cherish a profound love for each other in every moment, for love truly has the power to elevate every aspect of life. I love you more than words can say, and I'm excited to see what wonderful things happen in your life.

With all my love.

To My Dear Rachel

It's really hard to express how much you mean to me, and I often think about all the great times we've had together.

As your dad, I have loved watching you grow up. You were such a cute and well-behaved baby. You were such a good baby that you made us want to have more children, and we did.

As a child, you were caring, smart, determined, and always competing with your brother, Sean. I remember when you were little, you would make a special noise that melted my heart. That was our thing between us. I loved that so much.

While you were growing up, you were like a loving, caring, protective mother to your younger sisters, Michelle, and Casey. You always looked out for their well-being, and that made me so proud of you.

Growing up, you were the brightest student in all your classes. Your teachers loved you. Your classmates wanted to be your friends. As a soccer and volleyball player, everyone noticed you because you were one of the best. Your pure heart, beautiful smile, and charm caught people's attention. You were really good at sports. When you were eight, you used to wake up early every day to go running with me, and I was so proud of you for that. We spent time playing soccer together, and you always did everything I asked. You were an amazing soccer player.

As you grew up, you always excelled in your studies. Witnessing you complete your education, attend law school, become a lawyer, marry Richard, and welcome Richy boy and Ruby joon into your lives filled me with immense pride and joy.

Your marriage has brought wonderful additions to our family as well, including Richard's dear mom Karen, his dear sister Andrea, and her husband, Mark, along with their three lovely children Mark, Nora, and Teddy. Additionally, Richard's other dear sister Tammy and her husband Pete, with their three beautiful children Leo and twins Arthur and Gus, and Richards's youngest dear sister Lara and her husband, Chris, along with their two adorable children Johnny and Claire, have truly blessed our family.

You're an amazing mom, the way you spend all your time with your children is remarkable. I love you a lot, and I've always wished for your happiness, success, and well-being.

Watching you become the amazing adult you are today has been one of the best things in my life. I'm really proud of the person you've become and the path you've chosen.

You've faced challenges with courage, and I've seen you achieve amazing things. Your strength and determination inspire me, and I'm sure you'll keep doing great things.

Thank you for being such an incredible daughter! Thank you for brightening every day of my life.

Watching you grow to become a loving, patient mother to your own children has been the greatest joy of my life. It's the greatest achievement you'll ever make, and someday, you'll look back on today with the love and longing I feel for you now.

Your worth as a mother and my precious daughter is so much greater than anything the world has to offer. Cherish it as I cherish you.

I want you to know that my love for you is constant and unwavering. No matter where you are or what you're going through, you have my unconditional love and support.

Above all else, my dear Rachel and Richard, my greatest wish for both of you is to continue building a cozy and caring home together because it's the most important thing in life. Follow Christ's way of love; treat each other with kindness and respect, whether things are easy or tough. Be trustworthy and stay loyal to one another. But most importantly, love each other deeply through every moment. Love truly does make everything better. Real, godly love comes from seeking guidance and wisdom from God (you can find that in 1 Corinthians 13). Love means being patient and kind, not selfish or boastful. It involves showing respect and honor and steering clear of doing things that are hurtful or disrespectful. Instead, love focuses on what's good for others, gently guiding and celebrating truth and goodness. Hold onto each other tightly, and most importantly, hold onto your faith. That's what will keep your love strong and your home filled with warmth and care.

Your walk with the Lord, happiness, and well-being will always be my top priorities; and I'm here for you no matter what.

With all my love!

To My Dear Yasmin

I hope this letter finds you feeling loved and happy. As I think about our time together, I'm filled with gratitude for the special moments we've had.

Since you came into my life as a little girl, I've been amazed by your kindness, loyalty, intelligence, and humor. It meant a lot that you let me be like a father to you, and I thank you form the bottom of my heart for it.

Watching you grow into the amazing person you are today has been a privilege. Our family journey can be tricky, but your grace and understanding have made it a journey of love and growth.

Your presence has made our family even more special, and I cherish the bond we've built. Your laughter brings me joy, and your strength inspires me.

I remember when we had fun together, playing the game where we said the funniest things we knew. I would say things like "there are no cats in America" and "when it beeps, it's ready." It brought a smile to your face, and those moments are forever in my heart. I cherish them and miss them a lot.

Your success in school, college, and law school, and becoming a lawyer fills me with pride. Your resilience and optimism light the way for all of us, and your achievements show your determination and beautiful spirit.

Your wedding day with Eman was a special moment, and the arrival of Clara joon, with another on the way, added even more happiness. Your marriage has also brought lovely additions to our family. Each of them has become a cherished part of our family.

Your dedication to being an amazing mom is remarkable, and your efforts for Clara are truly commendable.

As I watch you grow into the remarkable person you are today, I am filled with awe and admiration. Your journey of self-discovery has been a privilege to witness. Through every triumph and setback, you have displayed resilience, determination, and grace.

Your ability to see the best in others and offer them comfort and solace is also remarkable. You have a heart that knows no bounds in helping others. I hope my love for you has played some part in the wondrous woman you've become.

As we continue, know that I will always love you in every step, I'm here beside you, cheering you on and loving you.

Above all else, my dear Yasmin and Eman, my greatest wish for both of you is to continue building a warm and caring home together because it's the most important thing in life. Follow Christ's path of love; treat each other with kindness and respect, whether things are easy or tough. Be trustworthy and stay loyal to one another. But most importantly, love each other deeply through every moment. Love truly makes everything better. True, godly love comes from seeking guidance and wisdom from God (you can find that in 1 Corinthians 13). Love means being patient and kind, not selfish or boastful. It involves showing respect and honor and avoiding actions that are hurtful or disrespectful. Instead, love focuses on what's good for others, gently guiding and celebrating truth and goodness. Thank you for being the wonderful individuals you are and gracing our lives. Here's to many more beautiful chapters together.

With all my love.

To My Dear Michelle

My heart overflows with love as I write this letter to you.

It feels like just yesterday when you were a precious newborn in my arms, and now you've become a wonderful, responsible woman making your mark on the world.

As a little one, you were absolutely adorable! Your curly hair was the cutest, and everyone loved it. You were so sweet, loving, caring, and kind. You brought a lot of happiness to everyone, especially our family. We adored you so much that sometimes you got away with a few things. Your excitement for life was so infectious! You loved playing with your siblings and putting on shows for us, and you were really good at it. We all loved those times together. They were full of happiness and will always be cherished in our hearts.

Watching you progress through school, graduate, and attend Pensacola Christian College has brought me great joy and pride, especially witnessing your deep walk with the Lord and your time working at TBC.

Observing your marriage to Jon right after college and witnessing you both become parents to the adorable Madi Joon and Mila joon brought tremendous joy to my heart. Jon's family, from his dear mom, Rose, to his late dad, Lary, has brought immense blessings to us. There's his oldest brother Josh and his wife, Hannah, along with their two lovely children, Cameron and Palin. We've warmly embraced Jon's dear sister Jamie, and his youngest brother Jake, who is married to Meghen, along with their adorable children, Nolan and Braden. They've all become treasured members of our family. I am impressed with how you have chosen to stay home and dedicate yourself to being the best parent you can be for your children.

It's been a privilege witnessing your journey to the person you are today. I want you to know how grateful I am to be your parent.

Since the day you were born, you brought love, laughter, and an unbreakable bond into my life. You've been a tremendous strength and inspiring hope in my heart.

Above all else, my dear Michelle and John, my greatest wish for both of you is to keep building a cozy and caring home together because it's the most important thing in life. Follow Christ's way of love; treat each other with kindness and respect, whether things are easy or tough. Be trustworthy and stay loyal to one another. But most importantly, love each other deeply through every moment. Love truly does make everything better. Real, godly love comes from seeking guidance and wisdom from God (you can find that in 1 Corinthians 13). Love means being patient and kind, not selfish or boastful. It involves showing respect and honor and steering clear of doing things that are hurtful or disrespectful. Instead, love focuses on what's good for others, gently guiding and celebrating truth and goodness. Thank you for being the remarkable person that you are. I have been blessed to be your parent, and I am excited to see where life takes you next.

Always remember that you are loved beyond measure. I love you endlessly, forever, and always.

With all my love and a heart full of pride.

To My Dear Casey

I hope this letter finds you surrounded by warmth and love. As I share my thoughts, my heart overflows with pride and gratitude for the amazing person you've become.

In those early days, you brought so much joy and laughter to everyone around you as a lovable baby. Those playful moments, the bond with your sisters, Sean, and acting in plays were truly special. You had so much fun creating funny positions during our "get into airplane crash positions" game, and those moments mean a lot to me. Our love for you knew no bounds because you were our world.

Your journey through life—marked by faith, strength, and resilience—has made you truly extraordinary. Gabe's arrival brought immense joy, and seeing you as a caring, loving mom fills my heart with happiness. I know it was tough when dear Jordan passed away, but Gabe is a precious blessing, and I'm thrilled that you have such a wonderful, kind, and smart son. Your story inspires everyone who knows you, radiating strength that leaves a lasting impact.

As you continue your journey, I wish for more growth, joy, and God's abundant blessings. I'm here, cheering you on and celebrating the amazing person you are.

I recently came across an article that reminded me of you, discussing nurturing a godly family as a single mom, much like your journey. This touched me because it aligns with the values I've tried to instill in you and your little family. From the beginning, my greatest desire has been to nurture your love for Jesus and support your spiritual growth. There were moments of concern about the absence of a husband and father figure, especially for Gabe. However, I've realized that despite the nontraditional family structure, you can embark on a meaningful faith journey together. While you can't fulfill both parental roles, you can exemplify godliness and impart valuable lessons about Jesus to your son.

Navigating this path has had its challenges, requiring adjustments within our family dynamic. But I'm convinced that the efforts we invest in deepening our spiritual connection are well worth it. Remember, it's not about possessions or worldly blessings. It's about having a personal relationship with God, as emphasized in John 17:3: "Eternal life means knowing you, the only true God, and Jesus Christ, whom you sent."

Casey, even though I may not fulfill all your expectations, know that I am wholeheartedly dedicated to supporting your family in becoming more like Christ. This journey is continuous, and while it may present difficulties, I have unwavering faith that God is with us every step of the way.

Stay true to yourself and to God. Don't be afraid to take risks and remember, it's okay to make mistakes—they serve as valuable lessons that shape your character and growth.

Always remember, I believe in you and your ability to achieve anything you put your mind to. Life will have its good and tough times, but I know you've got the strength and trust in God to handle anything. Whenever things get hard, know that you have support from God, family, friends, and others. We all believe in you and are here to support you. Trust in God and in yourself, and never stop pushing forward.

Follow the way of love that Christ showed us. True, godly love comes from seeking guidance and wisdom from God, as found in 1 Corinthians 13. Love means being patient and kind, prioritizing your family over yourself. It's all about treating others with respect and honor, avoiding hurtful or disrespectful actions. Instead, love aims to do good for others, gently guiding and celebrating what's true and good.

Hold on to your faith tightly. It's what will keep your love strong and your home full of warmth and care. You are such a good, caring, responsible, loving mom, and Gabe is blessed because of your love and care.

Remember the teachings of the Bible and don't ignore its advice. According to Proverbs 4:5–27, it advises not to turn away from wisdom, as it acts as a protection. Loving wisdom will keep you safe. Trust the Lord completely, and don't depend on your own thoughts and experiences. With every step you take, think about what He wants, and He will help you go the right way. Don't trust in your own wisdom, but fear and respect the Lord!

With all my love and endless support!

To My Beloved Grandchildren

Writing to my dearest grandchildren is important for several reasons:

The Bible teaches us to pass down wisdom, teachings, and blessings to the next generation. Writing to my cherished grandchildren follows these biblical values in several ways:

Legacy of faith. The Bible encourages sharing stories of faith and God's goodness with future generations (Psalm 78:4). This book allows me to pass on my faith, values, and experiences with God, strengthening their spiritual journey.

Teaching and guidance. Scripture highlights teaching and guiding children in the ways of the Lord (Deuteronomy 6:6–7). Through this book, I can share valuable life lessons, morals, and biblical principles to guide their lives.

Expressing love and blessings. The Bible emphasizes love for family and the blessing of generations (Proverbs 17:6). Writing this book expresses my love, care, and blessings upon them, making them feel cherished and valued. And showing God's love through my words.

Leaving a testament. Like biblical figures left messages, my book serves as a testament to our beliefs, values, and personal stories that can be treasured for generations to come. And life experiences, leaving behind a legacy of faith and love.

Encouragement and support. Encouragement is vital in the Bible (1 Thessalonians 5:11). My book aims to uplift and support them, guiding them through life's challenges with my love and God's guidance.

Preserving memories. By writing to them in this book, I preserve memories and experiences that I want to share with them, allowing them to understand their family's history and values.

Building relationships. Writing this book fosters a deeper connection and bond between me and my grandchildren, even if age and time separate us physically.

Creating lasting impressions. Letters to my grandchildren can create lasting impressions and positive memories that they will carry with them throughout their lives.

Lastly, by writing to my beloved grandchildren in this book, I aim to follow the Bible's teachings about passing down faith, love, wisdom, and blessings to future generations. This ensures a legacy firmly grounded in God's Word and love.

The Bible says in Proverbs 17:6 KJV,

Dear grandchildren and family, I want to share with everyone how much joy being with you and my grandkids brings to my heart. Whether it's birthdays, spending time together, taking care of them, holidays, sleepovers, or family trips, when all nine of them gather, it truly warms my heart. There are many things I cherish about being around my grandchildren—giving them hugs, holding them close, feeding them, playing games, reading stories, and especially talking with them on their level. These moments bring great joy to my soul, and I always look forward to spending time with them.

When our family gets together, little Richy, Nolan, Mila, Clara, and six-month-old Ruby in her baby rocker usually come to sit on my lap, pull on my jeans, and capture my attention with their toys—cars, stickers, and various games. They enthusiastically ask, "Play cars, play this with me, Grandpa or Bubba Joon?" It's all about playfulness while my other grandkids—Ethan, Gaby, Ellie, and Madi, aged three to ten—are running around the house, chasing each other, wrestling, screaming, laughing, etc., creating a lively atmosphere. Meanwhile, my adult children gather, sharing stories and catching up. The house is full of family, and I thank God from the bottom of my heart for this beautiful sight. Being around my family and grandkids fills me with immense joy.

Despite my busy schedule, before every family gathering, I take a moment to reflect on the loving and precious presence of Christ coming down to earth for us. This perspective has changed how I see things. I've decided that during these special moments, I will let go of tasks, set aside my lists, get on the floor, and play with gratitude. Grandkids teach us to play, wonder, and be free. Let's fully embrace that healing joy. I thank my Heavenly Father for blessing us with these carefree, creative, and colorful children.

> Children's children are the crown of old men; and the glory of children are their fathers.

My dearest grandchildren, Ethan boy, Ellie girl, Gaby boy, Madi joon, Nolan boy, Clara joon, Richy boy, Mila joon, and the little one arriving in April: I want you to feel the depth of my love for each of you. You brighten my life, and every moment together is treasured.

One day, when you're older and able to read this, I hope this book fills your hearts with blessings. As you grow into teens and adults, you'll encounter a world that's not always safe, and people who aren't always warm and cozy. The planet may be in a climate crisis, and society may have rich and poor people leading very different lives. There will be disappointments, hurt, and anger, as everyone faces challenges. You might experience heartbreak or struggle with health and financial issues. But dear grandchildren, I hope you always carry my values and love with you, like a locket close to your heart. Let this love remind you of your natural lovability and your inherent value. I want to encourage all of you to learn and understand the teachings of the Bible and not ignore its advice. In Proverbs 4:5–27, it advises not to turn away from wisdom, as it acts as a protection. Loving wisdom will keep you safe.

> The first step to being wise is to seek wisdom. Use everything you have to understand things better. Love wisdom, and it will make you great. Hold on to wisdom, and it will bring you

> honor. Wisdom will reward you with a crown of
> honor and glory.

Listen to me, dear grandkids. Follow my advice, and you'll live a long time. I'm teaching you about wisdom and guiding you on the right path. As you walk on it, you won't fall into traps, even if you run. Always remember this teaching; it's the key to life, so guard it well.

Don't choose the way of those who do wrong or evil things. Stay far away from it; don't even go near it. Turn around and go a different way. The people who do wrong things are always restless and looking to harm others. They thrive on doing bad things.

My dear grandkids, pay attention to what I say. Listen closely to my words. Don't let them out of your sight, and always think about them. These words are the secret to a good life and good health for those who discover them. *Above all, be careful about your thoughts because they control your life.*

Don't twist the truth or say things that are not right. Keep your eyes on the path, look straight ahead, and make sure you're going the right way. Nothing will make you fall if you don't go to the right or left. This way, you'll stay away from evil (Proverbs 4:10–23).

As you navigate through education, a career, and the complexities of love, remember that there are others less fortunate. I hope that when you're ready, you'll extend your hand, love, and positive gaze to them, giving back all that you've received.

Don't let others define and limit you. Remember, life doesn't happen on text. Don't let technology distract you from real human connections. It occurs in your family face-to-face, eye to eye, and skin to skin—outdoors in the sun and rain, woods, and oceans.

Research shows that teens spending more time looking at screens than being with friends and family feel lonelier and unhappier, not more connected. So, use your iPhones and iPads to serve you, not the other way around. Make sure your devices are not the last thing you see before going to bed or the first thing you see upon waking up. Instead, let the Bible, the Lord be that comforting presence for you. Jesus once said in Matthew 19:14 (KJV), "Let the little children come to me." That means Jesus loves kids like you and wants you close to Him.

As you grow in life, I wish only the best for you. May your days be filled with love, joy, and peace. When times are tough, I hope you find the strength to endure and the patience to overcome struggles. Be gentle, kindness is a special gift, both to yourselves and to others.

Let goodness be your compass and hold onto your faith in God's goodness. When things seem uncertain, embrace humility, for it brings inner strength. Remember to balance your actions with wisdom; it's the way to real freedom. Pursue your dreams boldly, knowing that love-filled hearts and hopeful spirits are unstoppable.

Know that my love for you never ends, and my support for you is unwavering. I'm here, always, no matter where life leads you. I'm proud of the incredible people you're becoming and excited to see all the amazing things you'll achieve.

May love, happiness, and success always fill your lives.

I'm putting pen to paper to share some vital life wisdom with you:

Advice from Grandpa, Bubba Joon

Life is like a roller-coaster ride—full of ups, downs, twists, and turns.

Kids, like you, are precious and unaware of life's harshness. You're also unaware of the incredible things that are possible. Life can be tough and sometimes unforgiving, but it's also filled with rewarding and amazing moments. There will be times of disappointment and heartache, but there will also be moments of great joy.

In our world today, there are many tough challenges—things like crime, war, and racism—that often make us wonder why evil exists. The Bible helps us understand this better. It talks about the devil, also known as Satan, who holds power in this world. Jesus said a time will come to judge this world, and Satan, the ruler here, will be cast out. The Bible also explains that Satan can cloud the minds of those who don't believe, making it hard for them to see the good news about Jesus.

Another source of evil is our human tendency toward doing wrong. The Bible says our hearts can be tricky and do bad things, but God sees our hearts and our actions.

I want you to know that you were created by a loving God, and you're so incredibly valuable. God loves you and wants a close relationship with you. Even if the world says we're just accidents, the Bible tells a different story. We were purposefully created by a loving God who knew us even before we came into this world. Each of us has a unique purpose, and the real joy comes from having a connection with God.

God knew you before you were born, and He knows everything about you. When you give your life to Him, He gives you a fresh start. God wants to be close to you because that's where life forever comes from.

God's love is so vast that He sent Jesus to sacrifice Himself for you. He loves you deeply and has an amazing plan for your lives.

Sometimes people think of God as far away or stern, but He's kind, gentle, and the most loving presence in the whole universe. God is love, and He's like the most caring Father to us all. His biggest wish is for you to know how much He loves you.

As your grandpa, just like your mom and dad, I also want to give you the best tools and wisdom to live your best life following good principles. When tough times come, remember that the Lord is by your side, and you can always turn to Him for help and support.

So dear grandchildren, here are a few important things I want you to know and live by:

1. *Always love.* Remember that God is love (1 John 4:8), and His love is unconditional. Embrace His love and share it with others.
2. *Be kind.* Show kindness and empathy to others, as people are drawn to those who are understanding, caring, and compassionate.

   Ephesians 4:32 KJV: "And be ye kind one to another, tenderhearted, forgiving one another. Always show kindness and empathy like your heavenly Father."

Treat others as you would want to be treated. This is the golden rule—Jesus said in Mathew 7:12 KJV—"Therefore all things whatsoever ye would that men should do to you, do ye even so to them: for this is the law and the prophets."

3. *Help others.* Bear one another's burdens and lend a helping hand to those in need (Galatians 6:2 KJV). "Bear ye one another's burdens, and so fulfill the law of Christ. Give. You get what you give, so be helpful and encouraging to others."
4. *Put your best effort.* Give your all to every task and remember that success is sweeter when you've worked hard for it. Proverbs 12:24 KJV says, "The hand of the diligent shall bear rule: but the slothful shall be under tribute." In another word, those who work hard will be put in charge of others, but lazy people will have to work like slaves. Go all in when you have a task to complete or a goal to achieve. Give 100 percent to any undertaking. Be happy about successes and know you are capable. Remember, no pain, no gain!
5. *Balance pride and humility.* Be proud of your accomplishments but remain humble and avoid unhealthy pride that seeks self-praise. Pride is a double-edged sword: It's normal to feel proud whenever we do something good, such as accomplishing a goal, becoming successful at something after all the effort and time we poured into it, obtaining something nice by buying it with our hard-earned money, doing something great for others, or feeling nice in general about our traits and qualities. It is considered authentic when pride comes from within and motivates us to improve.

Unhealthy pride happens when we do or say things for the purpose of people praising our SELF or for making our SELF feel good or for putting our SELF ahead of someone else's SELF. Pride wants our SELF to be praised, get glory, be worshiped, and be highly talked about, even when we're not in the room.

We read in Proverbs 11:12 NIV:

> When pride comes, then comes disgrace, but with humility comes wisdom.

> The fear of the Lord is to hate evil: pride, and arrogancy, and the evil way, and the froward mouth, do I hate. (Proverbs 8:13 KJV)

Have pride in your accomplishments. The prize is always sweeter when you've worked hard and scrambled to get there.

6. *Be humble!* Be completely humble and gentle; be patient, bearing one another in love. (Ephesians 4:2 NIV) Admit when you make a mistake. We are all human. We read in Romans 3:10 KJ. "As it is written, There is none righteous, no, not one." Start again and do it right next time.
7. *Have strength.* Trust in the Lord and find your strength in Him when faced with adversity. But those who hope in the Lord will renew their strength. They will soar on wings like eagles; they will run and not grow weary; they will walk and not faint (Isaiah 40:31 NIV).

   When things go wrong, and they probably will at some point, be strong and always remember the Lord. My flesh and my heart may fail, but God is the strength of my heart and my portion forever (Psalm 73:26 NIV).
8. *Be courageous!* Have I not commanded you? Be strong and courageous. Do not be afraid; do not be discouraged, for the Lord your God will be with you wherever you go (Joshua 1:9 NIV). Pick yourself up, dust off, and push ahead. As it is written in Philippians 4:13 KJV, "I can do all things through Christ which strengtheneth me." There will be highs and lows during your life. With the love of God, and support of your awesome family, and the perseverance and strength you have inside, you will be able to handle whatever comes your way.

9. *Be thirsty to learn.* Never stop learning and seek wisdom through reading the Word of God. Whatever you have learned or received or heard from me or seen in me—put it into practice. And the God of peace will be with you (Philippians 4:9 NIV). Learn, learn, learn. Psalm 25:4 KJV says, "Shew me thy ways, O Lord; teach me thy paths." It never ends. You will never know it all, even if you think you already do. There's that "one more thing" that could tip the scales in your favor. Don't miss out.
10. *Be open-minded.* Listen to advice and make your own decisions while practicing humility. Whoever gives heed to instruction prospers, and blessed is the one who trusts in the Lord (Proverbs 16:20 NIV). Therefore, everyone who hears these words of mine and puts them into practice is like a wise man who built his house on the rock (Matthew 7:24 NIV). Listen to advice from others, even if you don't agree with them. Consider their opinions but make your own decisions.
11. *Team up with the Lord.* Put your trust in the Lord and follow His path. Trust in the Lord with all your heart and lean not on your own understanding; in all your ways submit to him, and he will make your paths straight (Proverbs 3:5–6 NIV). Choose the right way, God's way and let it become your own way.

    The Lord is with you, and you oversee your own life. You are the one to live with your choices.
12. *Be involved.* Serve the Lord and make the world a better place. It is the Lord your God you must follow, and him you must revere. Keep his commands and obey him; serve him and hold fast to him (Deuteronomy 13:4 NIV). Walk in obedience to all that the Lord your God has commanded you, so that you may live and prosper and prolong your days in the land that you will possess (Deuteronomy 5:33 NIV).

    The Lord himself goes before you and will be with you; he will never leave you nor forsake you. Do not be afraid; do not be discouraged. (Deuteronomy 31:8 NIV) Make the world a better place. Matthew 5:14 KJV says,

"Ye are the light of the world. A city that is set on an hill cannot be hid." Always do right, fight, and support what is right. Romans 12:21 KJV says, "Be not overcome of evil, but overcome evil with good. "Do what you can to leave your mark—let them know you were here!"

13. *Find happiness in the Lord.* Ask and receive, and your joy will be complete in Him. Until now, you have not asked for anything in my name. Ask and you will receive, and your joy will be complete (John 16:24 NIV). I have told you this so that my joy may be in you and that your joy may be complete (John 15:11 NIV). Laugh. Enjoy your life. Have fun. Be happy. First Thessalonians 5:16 KJV says, "Rejoice evermore."
14. *Remember family.* Honor and cherish your family, for they are your pride and your support. Honor your father and your mother, so that you may live long in the land the Lord your God is giving you (Exodus 20:12 NIV).

    Grandchildren are the crowning glory of the aged; parents are the pride of their children (Proverbs 17:6 NIV).

These commandments that I give you today are to be on your hearts. Impress them on your children. Talk about them when you sit at home, and when you walk along the road when you lie down, and when you get up (Deuteronomy 6:6–7 NIV). Stay with your family, plan not to move out of the state, and spend time with your family. The love and support you have from them can't be measured.

Know Where You Came From

Learn all you can from the Bible, about your connections, traditions, and history

15. *Know your roots.* Learn about your heritage and traditions and read the Bible to gain insight into your faith.

Love God and pursue God! Jesus said in Mark 12:30 KJV, "And thou shalt love the Lord thy God with all thy heart, and with all thy soul, and with all thy mind, and with all thy strength: this is the first commandment."

Every day find a way to read the Word of God, worship, and love your God. Have faith in Him through all things.

> Thy words were found, and I did eat them; and thy word was unto me the joy and rejoicing of mine heart: for I am called by thy name, O LORD God of hosts. (Jeremiah 15:16)

Jeremiah treasured the Word of God in his heart and it became his joy and delight, and he readily received all that the Lord had to offer.

> Don't doubt, know that word of the Lord is pure and righteous altogether—and stands fast for ever and ever. (Psalm 19:7–9; Easy-to-Read Version)

The LORD's teachings are perfect. They give strength to his people. The LORD's rules can be trusted. They help even the foolish become wise. The LORD's laws are right. They make people happy. The LORD's commands are good. They show people the right way to live.

Learning respect for the LORD is good. It will last forever. The LORD's judgments are right. They are completely fair.

Here is one of the wonderful songs I enjoy playing in my car whenever I am driving you around. I hope you remember this song. It is a song that I often sing with you on every ride and trip. Its lyrics resonate deeply with me, and I feel the Holy Spirit touching my heart, and I hope it resonates with you too, so I would like to share it with you:

> O be careful little eyes what you see O be careful little eyes what you see For the Father up

above Is looking down in love So, be careful little eyes what you see

O be careful little ears what you hear O be careful little ears what you hear For the Father up above Is looking down in love So, be careful little ears what you hear

O be careful little tongue what you say O be careful little tongue what you say For the Father up above Is looking down in love So, be careful little tongue what you say

O be careful little hands what you do O be careful little hands what you do For the Father up above Is looking down in love So, be careful little hands what you do

O be careful little feet where you go O be careful little feet where you go For the Father up above Is looking down in love So, be careful little feet where you go

O be careful little heart whom you trust O be careful little heart whom you trust For the Father up above Is looking down in love So, be careful little heart whom you trust

O be careful little mind what you think O be careful little mind what you think For the Father up above Is looking down in love So, be careful little mind what you think So, be careful little mind what you think

(Copyright 1956 by Zondervan Music Publishers)

Dear grandchildren, in closing, always strive to seek God, to love Him, and to welcome His presence into your daily lives. Don't be afraid to open your hearts to the Lord.

1. *Always love.* Remember, God is all about love, and it's pretty special. Spread that love around to everyone.

2. *Be kind.* Treat others nicely, with care and understanding. Think about how you'd want to be treated and do the same for them.
3. *Help others.* When someone needs a hand, give them one. It's like a big circle—what you give, you get back.
4. *Try your best.* Whatever you do, put your heart into it. Success feels super awesome when you've put in the effort.
5. *Be proud, stay humble.* Feel good about your achievements, but never forget to stay down to earth and kind. Pride is great when it's not all about showing off.
6. *Stay humble.* Admit mistakes 'cause we all mess up sometimes. It's cool. Just try again next time.
7. *Stay strong.* Whenever things get tough, remember, you're never alone. Trust in something bigger than yourself.
8. *Be brave.* When life gets tricky, don't give up. You're stronger than you think. Keep going!
9. *Keep learning.* Never stop learning, especially from the good stuff you find in the Bible. There's always more to learn.
10. *Listen and decide.* Hear people out, even if you don't agree. But in the end, make your own choices.
11. *Trust God.* Follow the path you believe is right. Trusting in something bigger can guide you.
12. *Make the world better.* Do your part to make the world a better place. Fight for what's right and spread goodness.
13. *Find joy.* Laugh, have fun, and be happy. Life's too short not to enjoy it.
14. *Cherish family.* Your family's pretty awesome. Be good to them. They're your roots, and they love you.
15. *Know where you come from.* Learn about your family history and traditions. And remember, love and faith go a long way.

I hope these words stick with you and bring you joy as they've brought me. Stay true to yourselves!

With all my love.

Dear Heavenly Father,

Thank You for the lives of each of my lovely grandchildren that You have so graciously brought into my life. They all give me such joy and pleasure, for which I praise and thank You.

Dear Lord,

Thank You for Your written Word and for Jesus Christ, the living Word of God. I pray that Your Word would become for my grandchildren a joy and the delight of their hearts. Give them a heart to love you more every day and more than anything else. I pray that they may be a doer of the word and always trust in its precepts and promises, no matter what difficulties and dangers they may have to undergo as an individual or family. Help them to cling unto You and hold fast to that which is good and do only those things that are pleasing in Your sight. Grant them the blessing of a Godly family.

Thank You, again and again, Lord so much, for every one of my grandchildren. Into Your hands, I commit each one. May they sense Your calling on their lives, so that they develop into mighty men and women who love You deeply and trust in You implicitly.

In Jesus's name, I pray.

What Do I Want for My Children

Dear family and friends,

I wanted to take a moment to share something that's been on my heart lately—the importance of instilling in our children the values and teachings found in the Bible.

As a parent, I have come to realize how crucial it is to have a clear understanding of what we want for our children, guided by the wisdom of the Bible.

Here are a few reasons why I believe this is significant:

1. *Moral foundation.* The Bible provides a solid moral foundation centered around love, kindness, forgiveness, and empathy. These principles are invaluable in shaping our children's character and how they interact with the world around them.
2. *Spiritual growth.* Nurturing our children's spiritual growth is just as important as their academic or physical development. The teachings in the Bible offer guidance on faith, hope, and purpose, helping them find meaning in life beyond material pursuits.
3. *Resilience and perseverance.* In a world filled with challenges, the Bible encourages resilience, perseverance, and courage in the face of adversity. These teachings equip our children with the strength to overcome obstacles and stay true to their values.
4. *Building strong relationships.* Biblical values emphasize the importance of love, compassion, and community. Teaching

our children to embody these values fosters deeper and more meaningful relationships with others, contributing positively to society.

5. *Creating a positive impact.* Ultimately, guiding our children according to the Bible helps them become individuals who not only succeed in their personal endeavors but also positively impact the lives of others, making the world a better place.

I believe that by instilling these timeless principles in our children, we equip them to navigate life with wisdom, integrity, and purpose.

"As a parent, my deepest wish for my children is to see them thrive and grow into happy, compassionate, and resilient individuals. I want them to embrace life with curiosity, face challenges with courage, and find joy in their pursuits. I hope they cultivate strong values, empathy for others, and a sense of purpose. I want them to know they are unconditionally loved, supported, and cherished in their journey through life. Above all, I want them to walk with Him, I want them to be like Him!" Yes, it is my heart's desire that our children learn to love and serve the Lord with all their hearts, souls, and minds to bring Him honor and glory all the days of their lives.

Long ago, I heard a beautiful song from Pastor's wife, Susan Pitman back in 1996, called: "What Do I Want for My Children?" Immediately, the Holy Spirit made that song stick to my heart and caused me to make it as my goal for my children. I knew then that's what I wanted for my children.

Today I am a grandfather who has been blessed with five children and nine grandchildren, soon-to-be ten little ones. What is it that I want for my children? I think this song sums it up beautifully:

What do I want for my children?
What do I want for my children?
Do I seek for them world-wide fame?
Do I treasure for them wealth and riches?
Do I want their lives to be just like a game?

What do I want for my children?
Is it power and wisdom and might?
Do I want for them untold blessings?
Do I want everything to go just right?
I tell you what I want for my children, a heart full of peace from above,
A life of serving others, a heart of patience and love.
I want them to know my Savior, to be free from the power of sin.
This is what I want for my children,
I want them to walk with Him; I want them to be like Him!

Train up a child in the way he should go and when he is old, he will not depart from it. (Proverbs 22:6)

Reasons Behind This Book

Writing a book specifically addressed to my family and friends, titled "Do You Know for Sure God the Father Has Your Back," can be important for several reasons:

1. *Personal connection.* Addressing a book directly to my family and friends creates a personal connection. It shows that I care deeply about their spiritual well-being and am sharing something significant with them.
2. *Spiritual assurance.* The book's title suggests a focus on providing assurance about God's presence and support in one's life. In times of uncertainty or doubt, this assurance can offer comfort and guidance to my loved ones.
3. *Sharing personal insights.* My book contains personal stories, experiences, or insights that can resonate deeply with my family and friends. Sharing my journey and lessons learned could help them navigate their own spiritual paths.
4. *Encouragement and support.* Writing this book with a focus on faith can serve as a source of encouragement and support for my family and friends. It might provide guidance on how to strengthen their relationship with God and navigate life's challenges.
5. *Opening dialogue.* Sometimes, discussions about faith and spirituality can be challenging. My book allows me to articulate my beliefs, initiating a conversation that might be harder to start in person.

6. *Leaving a legacy.* Creating a book tailored to my loved ones can serve as a lasting legacy. It's a way to pass down my beliefs, values, and wisdom to future generations within my family and friend circle.
7. *Deepening relationships.* Sharing this book which is focused on faith can deepen my relationships with those closest to me. It offers a shared experience and an opportunity to connect on a deeper level.

> I'm writing this book for my beloved family and friends to share vital teachings from the Bible. These lessons focus on open communication, sharing wisdom, expressing love and support, leaving a lasting legacy, and providing guidance rooted in biblical teachings.

Passing on a biblical legacy to my family, friends, and everyone else is deeply important to me. It's both an honor and a responsibility. The story of Adam and Eve reveals how crucial this legacy is and how its loss can lead to tragedy, like what happened with Cain.

After Adam and Eve disobeyed God, He taught them His laws and rules, emphasizing the importance of passing down this wisdom to future generations. This passing on of beliefs and teachings forms the core of a biblical legacy.

God's grace helps me understand that teaching this legacy is not a choice; it is crucial. It is not something open for debate or change, even among shifting cultures. It serves as a defense against negative influences in society, rooted in timeless laws and teachings of God.

For more than thirty years, I've studied the Bible and lived by its teachings. I grasp how the serpent in the Bible tried to erase Adam and Eve's legacy, and I'm watchful for similar threats today.

I'm aware that some societal ideas contradict this biblical legacy:

- Some school materials may oppose respecting parents.
- Some governments aim for more control over what kids learn.
- There's a growing gap between generations.

- Certain individuals openly mock religious beliefs, trying to belittle them.

However, I remain steadfast, focusing on God's teachings, avoiding what goes against them, and encouraging goodness and wisdom among my family, friends, and everyone.

The Bible provides guidance on establishing this legacy:

> *When your son asketh thee in time to come, saying, What mean the testimonies, and the statutes, and the judgments, which the Lord our God hath commanded you? Then thou shalt say unto thy son…* (Deuteronomy 6:20–21)

The Bible is clear in Deuteronomy 6:1–19 KJV

> Now these are the commandments, the statutes, and the judgments, which the LORD your God commanded to teach you, that ye might do them in the land whither ye go to possess it:
>
> That thou mightest fear the LORD thy God, to keep all his statutes and his commandments, which I command thee, thou, and thy son, and thy son's son, all the days of thy life; and that thy days may be prolonged.
>
> Hear therefore, O Israel, and observe to do it; that it may be well with thee, and that ye may increase mightily, as the LORD God of thy fathers hath promised thee, in the land that floweth with milk and honey.
>
> Hear, O Israel: The LORD our God is one LORD:
>
> And thou shalt love the LORD thy God with all thine heart, and with all thy soul, and with all thy might.

And these words, which I command thee this day, shall be in thine heart:

And thou shalt teach them diligently unto thy children, and shalt talk of them when thou sittest in thine house, and when thou walkest by the way, and when thou liest down, and when thou risest up.

And thou shalt bind them for a sign upon thine hand, and they shall be as frontlets between thine eyes.

And thou shalt write them upon the posts of thy house, and on thy gates.

And it shall be, when the LORD thy God shall have brought thee into the land which he sware unto thy fathers, to Abraham, to Isaac, and to Jacob, to give thee great and goodly cities, which thou buildedst not,

And houses full of all good things, which thou filledst not, and wells digged, which thou diggedst not, vineyards and olive trees, which thou plantedst not; when thou shalt have eaten and be full;

Then beware lest thou forget the LORD, which brought thee forth out of the land of Egypt, from the house of bondage.

Thou shalt fear the LORD thy God, and serve him, and shalt swear by his name.

Ye shall not go after other gods, of the gods of the people which are round about you;

(For the LORD thy God is a jealous God among you) lest the anger of the LORD thy God be kindled against thee, and destroy thee from off the face of the earth.

Ye shall not tempt the LORD your God, as ye tempted him in Massah.

> Ye shall diligently keep the commandments of the LORD your God, and his testimonies, and his statutes, which he hath commanded thee.
>
> And thou shalt do that which is right and good in the sight of the LORD: that it may be well with thee, and that thou mayest go in and possess the good land which the LORD sware unto thy fathers.
>
> To cast out all thine enemies from before thee, as the LORD hath spoken.

In our world today, we face numerous challenges and complex societal issues, including various forms of wrongdoing such as crime, war, terrorism, racism, and more. These issues often seem to reinforce each other, creating a troubling cycle that makes us wonder why evil persists.

The most crucial issue in our lives is our relationship with God. This book respectfully challenges you to determine, without any doubt, whether you are right or wrong in your relationship with God. I want everyone to understand the rewards and joys that come with being right in this life and throughout eternity, as well as the consequences in this life and throughout eternity that come with being wrong.

According to the Bible, evil originates from two primary sources. The first is the devil, also known as Satan, who exercises significant influence in the world.

As mentioned in John 12:31 (NLT), Jesus indicated that a time for judgment had come, when Satan, the ruler of this world, would be cast out. Additionally, 2 Corinthians 4:4 (NLT) explains that Satan, as the god of this world, blinds the minds of unbelievers, preventing them from understanding the message of Christ.

The second source of evil is the inclination of the human heart toward sin and wickedness. Jeremiah 17:9–10 (NLT) describes the human heart as "the most deceitful of all things and desperately wicked." God, as the examiner of our hearts, rewards people based on their actions. It's essential to recognize that God is not the cause of evil but rather the solution to it.

My motivation for writing this book stems from several concerns:

1. Our current educational system and its impact on what our children learn.
2. The decline in faith among many children.
3. The influences and offerings of the world on our children and the next generation.
4. Risks in the digital world affecting our children.
5. The pursuit of truth, the way, and life itself.

We are accountable for safeguarding our children both in the online realm and from the outside world. They need our guidance because they cannot handle it alone and they do not know what they're getting themselves into.

Here's a glimpse of what our kids face online.

Bark, an online monitoring tool, processed 5.6 billion activities in 2023 across texts, email, YouTube, and various apps. They found the following:

- Self-harm/suicide: 33 percent of tweens / 57 percent of teens involved.
- Sexual content: 58 percent of tweens / 75 percent of teens encountered it.
- Anxiety: 19 percent of tweens / 36 percent of teens exposed to language about anxiety.
- Drugs/alcohol: 58 percent of tweens / 77 percent of teens talked about it.
- Bullying: 67 percent of tweens / 76 percent of teens experienced it.
- Depression: 26 percent of tweens / 38 percent of teens discussed it.
- Disordered eating: 9 percent of tweens / 21 percent of teens encountered it.

- Predators: 8 percent of tweens / 10 percent of teens faced online predatory behaviors.
- Violence: 68 percent of tweens / 82 percent of teens expressed or experienced violent thoughts.

In the past year, over forty states filed legal action against social media companies for designing addictive products that harm youth mental health. Despite some progress, there's still a lot of work to be done. In 2019, the National Center for Missing & Exploited Children received 16.9 million reports of child sexual abuse material. In 2022, this number nearly doubled to over 32 million reports.

(I gathered this information from "Enough is Enough," a national nonpartisan, nonprofit organization that has been at the forefront of advocating for a safer Internet for children and families since 1994).

Recent changes in our educational system, such as the elimination of homework and textbooks in elementary and middle schools, raise questions about what children are truly learning. Our society often pushes us to grow up quickly, aiming for independence, self-sufficiency, and self-made success. While these achievements have practical benefits, there's an alternative path to genuine greatness in the Kingdom of God.

In Matthew 18, Jesus's disciples debated who would be the greatest in God's kingdom, pondering whether it would be the most educated, the most religious, or the most disciplined. Jesus introduced a different perspective, emphasizing that becoming like little children is the key to greatness in God's Kingdom. Childlike humility and faith are of immense value.

The changes in our educational system reflect various commitments about what children should learn. Some prioritize academic preparation, while others emphasize social-emotional development and community values. However, in some cases, parents may not be fully aware of their children's curriculum.

The erosion of the concept of absolute truth is another significant concern. While the world claims that truth is relative and depends on time and social context, the Bible asserts that truth is unchanging. Some humanist teachings deny the existence of absolutes, leading to a disregard for God's timeless moral law.

Furthermore, the denial of God's role in creation is a growing issue. Some educational ideologies dismiss the idea of a Creator in favor of naturalistic explanations. The intricate design of the universe suggests an intelligent Creator, and it requires more faith to believe in randomness than in an Almighty God.

The normalization of vices like drinking and substance abuse among young people is concerning. Teenagers may be tempted into harmful activities with phrases like "a little drink or smoke won't hurt you." We must teach our children that they have an enemy seeking to harm them and that Jesus offers protection. They should honor their bodies as temples of God.

Modesty, which may be seen as old-fashioned, remains biblically important. Our culture is often influenced by media that promotes immodesty, but the Bible instructs women to be modest in their dress and behavior. It's crucial to instill the value of modesty in our children.

There's a prevailing belief that the government should take care of everyone, which aligns with a socialist mindset that has infiltrated educational institutions. While governments maintain law and order, they are not meant to fulfill every individual's needs. We must teach our children the importance of self-reliance and hard work.

Lastly, there's a growing misconception that all paths lead to heaven, undermining the exclusivity of Jesus Christ as the way to salvation. It's essential to emphasize Jesus as "the way, the truth, and the life," as stated in John 14:6. Not all paths lead to heaven, and it's our responsibility to communicate this truth to our children.

In a world where absolutes are questioned, our faith is challenged, and the truth is distorted, it is our duty as parents and guardians to guide our children and equip them with the knowledge and wisdom to navigate life's complexities.

We must serve as protectors of our children, nurturing their understanding of God's truth and the values that will lead them to a meaningful and purposeful life.

Over the past four-plus years, teaching in so many schools *have turned into an "humanist teaching"!*

Here are a few examples:

1. There is no absolute truth.

Please understand that in this world, there is the spirit of truth and the spirit of error!

We read this in 1 John 4:6 KJV: "We are of God: he that knoweth God heareth us; he that is not of God heareth not us. Hereby know we the spirit of truth, and the spirit of error."

Satan's demonic plan for man has been to destroy the absolutes. God's Word is absolute. Satan challenged it in the garden of Eden, and unfortunately, as far as mankind is concerned, Satan was highly successful.

We read in Psalms 117:2 KJV.

> *For his merciful kindness is great toward us: and the truth of the LORD endureth forever. Praise ye the LORD.*

The truth of the LORD endures forever. It never changes.

> *For the word of the LORD is right; and all his works are done in truth* (Psalms 33:4).

The Word of the LORD is right.

> *He is the Rock, his work is perfect: for all his ways are judgment: a God of truth and without iniquity, just and right is he.* (Deuteronomy 32:4)

All of God's work is perfect.

> *For I am the LORD, I change not; therefore ye sons of Jacob are not consumed.* (Malachi 3:6)

Our God does not change. His law does not change. His words do not change. His language does not change. His clothing does not change.

Humanist teachings say, "There are no absolutes; truth is relative to time and social settings, and the Bible doesn't pertain to this modern world."

Now, *the record.*

Truth never changes; it is absolute. Two thousand years ago, a man drove up in a chariot and committed adultery; today, he drives up in a car. The mode of transport has changed, but not the motivation. No matter how many years pass, the nature of evil remains constant. The moral law of God and the truth of His Word never change. It is just as powerful and consequential today as it was when it was declared to man from the very beginning of time. Those who refuse its directives will reap their sowing. There is no escape from this truth. The driving focus of Satan is to destroy the absolutes of God's Word, the world's only source of truth.

Satan appears to be a very tolerant god—the god of this world (2 Corinthians 4:4). With Satan, it's fine if you're a follower of Buddha or Mohammed or Hinduism or Confucianism. You can be a Satanist, a witch, an agnostic, or an atheist. All the above and much more are endorsed by Satan. The only thing that's off-limits is *the truth.*

Truth is God, and Satan is positioned exactly opposite to him. God is life; Satan is death. God is light; Satan is darkness. God is good; Satan is evil. God is love; Satan is hate. God is faith; Satan is unbelief.

Always keep in mind that there is one common denominator that exists in all the positions Satan endorses. That common denominator is rebellion against the word of God. Every position erected against the truth is simply a position of rebellion. There is no place for rebellion or stubbornness in the life of a child of God. Rebellion is Satan's oneness, just as obedience is God's oneness—just opposite ends of the measure.

We read in 1 Samuel 15:23:

> For rebellion is as the sin of witchcraft, and stubbornness is as iniquity and idolatry. Because

> thou hast rejected the word of the LORD, he hath also rejected thee from being king.

Jesus Christ defines truth in John 17:17: "*Sanctify them through thy truth: thy word is truth.*" Truth is absolute and has zero tolerance for anything that disagrees with it. Truth knows no opinion. Truth leaves no room for private interpretation. The truth, in fact, is its own interpretation.

When you understand, as Jesus said, that God's Word is Truth, it brings you to another profound understanding, which is found in John 1:1:

> In the beginning was the Word, and the Word was with God, and the Word was God.

God is a spirit, and the Word of God is, in fact, God. Words are spiritual. For God to accept something other than truth would be to deny himself and destroy truth...the absolutes. There can be no compromise. Truth is absolute in every way. Truth is constant, and God is truth.

We read in James 1:17:

> Every good gift and every perfect gift is from above, and cometh down from the Father of lights, with whom is no variableness, neither shadow of turning.

There is not even a shadow of a suggestion of compromise. Truth cannot change and still remain true. The passage of time does not change the truth. What God hated when the words were written remains constant.

Remember, you cannot add or take away from the truth and still have truth remain truth.

We read in Revelation 22:18–19:

> For I testify unto every man that heareth the words of the prophecy of this book, If any man

> shall add unto these things, God shall add unto him the plagues that are written in this book: And if any man shall take away from the words of the book of this prophecy, God shall take away his part out of the book of life, and out of the holy city, and from the things, which are written in this book.

God's truth always remains true.

The moment we accepted the ideology of *no absolute truth*, we lost the ability to discern right from wrong, and our situation determines our ethics, which sets aside the biblical truth.

Our children are exposed to humanist teachings: *"It's okay to lie, cheat, steal, do immorality,* commit sexual sin, be morally bad, do all kinds of shameful things, take part in witchcraft, hate people, cause trouble, be jealous, angry or selfish, causing people to argue and divide into separate groups, being filled with envy, getting drunk, having wild parties, and doing other things like this…it is okay if you have a good reason."

But God teaches in the Ten Commandments that thou shall not do them: "Jesus saith unto him, I am the way, the truth, and the life: no man cometh unto the Father but by me" (John 14:6 KJV).

2. Humanist teachings—God has nothing to do with creation.

I'm writing, and books don't just happen. Gowns and dresses don't evolve. Cakes and paintings have recipes and rules. Then you want me to believe something as complex as our universe just happened? That requires more faith than it does to believe there is a Sovereign Creator—an Almighty God.

People and their theories have hijacked our educational system, kicked God from the classroom, and force-fed our kids' ideologies. Why? We're too busy. It's been easier to give others complete access to the hearts and minds of our children than to educate ourselves and stand as watchmen for our children.

We read in Romans 1:19–20 KJV:

> Because that which may be known of God is manifest in them; for God hath shewed it unto them. For the invisible things of him from the creation of the world are clearly seen, being understood by the things that are made, even his eternal power and Godhead; so that they are without excuse.

3. Humanist teachings—a little drink or smoke won't hurt you.

Have you ever known anyone who desired to become an alcoholic or an addict? No, me either. But it happens every day when kids have too much time and money, little supervision, few rules, and no accountability. Teens believe they're invincible, but many learn they're not.

"Everybody's doing it" is an argument meant to entice our kids to participate in harmful activities. Satan is baiting his hook like a fisherman, waiting for our kid to nibble so he can set the hook and reel them in. And his bait and hooks are everywhere.

We must teach our kids they have an enemy who desires to destroy them. But Jesus will protect them if they understand their bodies are the temple of God. He loves them and has a good plan for their lives—even if they've messed up. That's why Jesus died—just for them!

> For I know the thoughts that I think toward you, saith the LORD, thoughts of peace, and not of evil, to give you an expected end. (Jeremiah 29:11 KJV)

4. Humanist teachings—modesty is an old-fashioned rule.

Yes, you can. But does how you act and what you wear honor God?

What's a parent to do? Between TV, movies, magazines, and social media, how can we raise modest teens? Is the command for girls and ladies to be modest old-fashioned? If we use the media as a guide, it will surely seem so. But that's not what the Word says. If our hearts are humble before God, everything else falls in line with His order.

God instructs women to be modest in their dress, in their actions, and reactions. What does the content of your closet illustrate about you? Modesty doesn't mean you must wear plain clothing, but it does mean the clothes you wear should cover your body.

> And I want the women to make themselves attractive in the right way. Their clothes should be sensible and appropriate. They should not draw attention to themselves with fancy hairstyles or gold jewelry or pearls or expensive clothes. (1 Timothy 2:9 ERV)

> It is not fancy hair, gold jewelry, or fine clothes that should make you beautiful. No, your beauty should come from inside you—the beauty of a gentle and quiet spirit. That beauty will never disappear. It is worth very much to God. (1 Peter 3:3–4 ERV)

5. Humanist teachings—it's the government's job to take care of everybody.

The storm of socialism roared into the college classroom years ago. Now it's crept into middle and high schools. Like my children's schoolbooks over thirty years ago, it only takes one generation to change a culture. And it looks like those who've replaced God are right on target.

God established governments to keep law and order in the land and to protect the country's citizens. We have raised a generation of kids who believe they are to be taken care of. We haven't taught them to work hard or allowed them to gain wisdom by suffering consequences, nor have we allowed them to learn the difference between wants and needs. May God have mercy on us.

> Let every person be subjected to the governing authorities. For there is no authority except from God, and those which exist are established by God... For because of this you also pay taxes, for rulers are servants of God, devoting themselves to this very thing. (Romans 13:1 and 6 NAS)

6. Humanist teachings—we can all be on different paths to heaven.

God has become a feel-good word in this generation. But the Lord Jesus Christ is a stone of stumbling. When the name of Jesus comes into the conversation, you've struck a nerve.

Jesus told us it would be this way. It's time to be precise in our words of witness. All paths do not lead to heaven. Jesus was clear and concise about who He is and who we are in Him.

> Jesus answered, "I am the way, the truth, and the life. The only way to the Father is through me." (John 14:6 KJV)

Heavenly Father's Love Letter

One of the best meaningful articles that I have ever read regarding God the Father and the Holy Spirit touched my heart, for it was the "Father's Love Letter" from 1999 Father Heart Communications FathersLoveLetter.com!

I quote, it says:

God Loves YOU.

And He is the Father you have been looking for
all your life. This is His love Letter to you.

You may not know me, but I know everything about you.
Psalm 139:1

I know when you sit down and when you rise up.
Psalm 139:2

I am familiar with all your ways.
Psalm 139:3

Even the very hairs on your head are numbered.
Matthew 10:29–31

For you were made in my image.
Genesis 1:27

In me you live and move and have your being.
Acts 17:28

For you are my offspring.
Acts 17:28

I knew you even before you were conceived.
Jeremiah 1:4–5
I chose you when I planned creation.
Ephesians 1:11–12

You were not a mistake, for all your days are written in my book.
Psalm 139:15–16

I determined the exact time of your birth and where you would live.
Acts 17:26

You are fearfully and wonderfully made.
Psalm 139:14

I knit you together in your mother's womb.
Psalm 139:13

And brought you forth on the day you were born.
Psalm 71:6

I have been misrepresented by those who don't know me.
John 8:41–44

I am not distant and angry but am the complete expression of love.
1 John 4:16

And it is my desire to lavish my love on you.
1 John 3:1

Simply because you are my child and I am your Father.
1 John 3:1

I offer you more than your earthly father ever could.
Matthew 7:11

For I am the perfect father.
Matthew 5:48

Every good gift that you receive comes from my hand.
James 1:17

For I am your provider and I meet all your needs.
Matthew 6:31–33

My plan for your future has always been filled with hope.
Jeremiah 29:11

Because I love you with an everlasting love.
Jeremiah 31:3

My thoughts toward you are countless as the sand on the seashore.
Psalm 139:17–18

And I rejoice over you with singing.
Zephaniah 3:17

I will never stop doing good to you.
Jeremiah 32:40

For you are my treasured possession.
Exodus 19:5

I desire to establish you with all my heart and all my soul.
Jeremiah 32:41

And I want to show you great and marvelous things.
Jeremiah 33:3

If you seek me with all your heart, you will find me.
Deuteronomy 4:29

Delight in me and I will give you the desires of your heart.
Psalm 37:4

For it is I who gave you those desires.
Philippians 2:13

I am able to do more for you than you could possibly imagine.
Ephesians 3:20

For I am your greatest encourager.
2 Thessalonians 2:16–17

I am also the Father who comforts you in all your troubles.
2 Corinthians 1:3–4

When you are brokenhearted, I am close to you.
Psalm 34:18

As a shepherd carries a lamb, I have carried you close to my heart.
Isaiah 40:11

One day I will wipe away every tear from your eyes.
Revelation 21:3–4

And I'll take away all the pain you have suffered on this earth.
Revelation 21:3–4

I am your Father, and I love you even as I love my son, Jesus.
John 17:23

For in Jesus, my love for you is revealed.
John 17:26

He is the exact representation of my being.
Hebrews 1:3

He came to demonstrate that I am for you, not against you.
Romans 8:31

And to tell you that I am not counting your sins.
2 Corinthians 5:18–19

Jesus died so that you and I could be reconciled.
2 Corinthians 5:18–19

His death was the ultimate expression of my love for you.
1 John 4:10

I gave up everything I loved that I might gain your love.
Romans 8:31–32

If you receive the gift of my son Jesus, you receive me.
1 John 2:23

And nothing will ever separate you from my love again.
Romans 8:38–39

Come home and I'll throw the biggest party heaven has ever seen.
Luke 15:7
I have always been Father, and will always be Father.
Ephesians 3:14–15

My question is… Will you be my child?
John 1:12–13

I am waiting for you.
Luke 15:11–3

Love, Your Dad
My Child,

Father's Love Letter
An intimate message from God to you.
Almighty God

1999 Father Heart Communications—FathersLoveLetter.
com—Please feel free to copy and share with others.

Understanding God Got Your Back

Truth Discovers

Understanding that "God got your back" is essential for various reasons:

1. *Comfort in challenges.* Life often presents challenges, and knowing that God supports and protects you can bring immense comfort. It helps you face difficulties with courage and hope.
2. *Trust and faith.* Believing that God has your back fosters trust and faith in His plans. Even in uncertain times, this understanding can anchor you and help you stay steadfast.
3. *Reducing anxiety.* Recognizing God's support can ease anxiety and fear about the future. It brings a sense of security, knowing that you're not alone in facing life's uncertainties.
4. *Guidance and direction.* Understanding that God is looking out for you allows you to seek His guidance and direction in life's decisions. Trusting in His support can lead to wiser choices.
5. *Strength in adversity.* During tough times, knowing that God has your back can provide the strength to endure and overcome challenges. It instills resilience and perseverance.

6. *Spiritual growth.* This understanding encourages spiritual growth by deepening your relationship with God. It prompts you to seek Him more earnestly and rely on His wisdom.
7. *Gratitude and peace.* Acknowledging God's support leads to gratitude, fostering a sense of peace and contentment in your life circumstances.
8. *Sense of purpose.* It reinforces the belief that you are part of a larger plan and that God's support ensures you're moving toward a purposeful life.

Ultimately, understanding that God "has your back" brings a sense of connection, purpose, and strength, shaping your perspective and responses to life's challenges.

Why should I forgive?

Did you know forgiveness is a command from God that shouldn't be taken lightly? Living with bitterness isn't a good way to live, and dying with it is even worse. But why should we forgive those who hurt us?

The way we treat others shows how we relate to God. Jesus takes it personally when we mistreat others. Being at odds with a fellow believer means being at odds with Christ in them. Similarly, our treatment of others reflects our attitude toward Christ.

Forgiveness is so crucial that Jesus highlighted it in the model prayer. He made it clear in Matthew 6:14–15: if we forgive others, God will forgive us. But if we don't forgive others, God won't forgive us either. Our treatment of others matters to God in how He treats us.

The model prayer guides us on how to talk to God. But before we speak with Him, we must address forgiveness: asking for forgiveness from God ("Forgive us our debts") is key.

Admitting and confessing our sins to God is essential for maintaining our relationship with Him. We need to be honest about our wrongdoings to restore our connection with God.

After asking for vertical forgiveness from God, we're reminded to forgive others horizontally. People forgiven by God should also be forgiving. As we receive God's forgiveness, we become capable of forgiving others. True grace extends forgiveness outwardly.

Our relationship with others is essential to God, even more than giving or serving. Jesus emphasized reconciling with others before offering gifts to God. Our service to God is unacceptable if we're personally contaminated by broken relationships.

The word "reconciliation" means being at peace with someone. Similarly, we need peace with God. Reconciliation is about making things right when they've gone wrong. When we offend someone, it's our responsibility to seek reconciliation, regardless of their response.

Unforgiveness and strained relationships affect our relationship with God. Jesus made forgiveness a priority because it affects how we relate to God. It's crucial, and subsequent chapters will delve deeper into the consequences of not forgiving.

"And forgive us our debts, as we forgive our debtors" (Matthew 6:12). This first part of the model prayer addresses vertical forgiveness: *"Forgive us our debts"* (Matthew 6:12).

Keeping short accounts with God by admitting and confessing our sins is imperative:

> If we say that we have fellowship with him, and walk in darkness, we lie, and do not the truth: But if we walk in the light, as he is in the light, we have fellowship one with another, and the blood of Jesus Christ his Son cleanseth us from all sin. If we say that we have no sin, we deceive ourselves, and the truth is not in us. If we confess our sins, he is faithful and just to forgive us our sins, and to cleanse us from all unrighteousness. (1 John 1:6–9)

"I have got your back." That is a saying we, as athletes and coaches, use often. We use it to describe our relationship with our teammates or players. It means we are in this together. It means that no one is alone. If something happens, we will be there to help each other out. This phrase also means that we are not alone. Our teammates "have our back." They are there to help us out. Help us up off the ground. Encourage us. Teach us. Work with us. But what happens when they are not there? The truth is the most well-meaning, kind-hearted teammate we have can't be there for us in every situation in life.

When life gets tough, and you're facing challenges like the death of a loved one, divorce, bankruptcy, or despair, who do you turn to for support? What happens when you're emotionally drained, depressed, and can't find your strength? When you're spiritually attacked, where do you run for assistance?

In these moments, it's easy to seek relief in the wrong places, like drugs, alcohol, or unhealthy relationships. But the Bible reminds us that God has our back. Prayer remains a powerful force, and the Holy Spirit continues to work in our lives. God honors the praises of His people, and His blessings are still pouring out.

Even when life seems overwhelming, we can find comfort in remembering that God is in control. The Word of the Lord endures forever, and Jesus, with all power in heaven and earth, is with us always. As we face life's challenges, we can turn to God, who has our back and offers guidance and strength.

Remember the words of Matthew 28:20, "Teaching them to observe all things whatsoever I have commanded you: and, lo, I am with you always, even unto the end of the world. Amen."

So when we are in trouble in life, of course, various people and support systems can have our back, such as family, friends, mentors, and even professional organizations or community groups. Here are the hows:

1. *Family.* Family members are often the first line of support. They provide emotional and financial assistance and can be a source of love and understanding during difficult times.
2. *Friends.* True friends stand by you in good times and bad. They offer emotional support, lend a listening ear, and sometimes practical help when needed.

3. *Mentors.* Mentors or role models can guide you through challenging situations. Their wisdom and advice can be invaluable when you're facing difficulties.
4. *Community.* Community support can come from local organizations, religious groups, or cultural communities. These groups often provide a sense of belonging and assistance during crises.
5. *Professionals.* In some situations, professionals like therapists, counselors, or doctors can offer specialized help for emotional, mental, or physical troubles.
6. *Government and social services.* Government agencies and social services can provide assistance, especially in cases of financial hardship, unemployment, or emergencies.
7. *Online communities.* In the digital age, online forums and social media groups can offer support and resources for people facing various challenges.
8. *Nonprofit organizations.* Many nonprofits are dedicated to helping those in need, whether it's related to health, education, poverty, or specific issues like addiction.
9. *Self-Help and resilience.* Sometimes, individuals find strength within themselves through self-help resources, personal growth, and building resilience.
10. *Pets.* The companionship of pets can also provide comfort and support during tough times. They offer unconditional love and emotional stability.

I want to remind you that the level of support and who provides it can vary greatly depending on the nature of the trouble we're facing. Each of these support systems plays a unique role in helping individuals navigate life's challenges.

There are moments when we find ourselves facing challenges alone, without anyone to support us. These are times when we must pick ourselves up and press forward, even when it seems there's no one physically present to assist us. Such moments can be stressful and uncomfortable, leaving us longing for help.

In my life, I have discovered an unwavering source of support, someone who always has my back in every situation: God, our Heavenly Father. The knowledge that God is watching over me provides a profound sense of calm and peace.

Changing ourselves to become happier and more honest-to-goodness human beings is a desire many of us share. When facing emotional problems like guilt, grief, loneliness, or stress, and dealing with negative attitudes, we often rely on our own reactions and solutions instead of turning to the Lord.

To change and overcome these challenges, it's essential to examine ourselves. Are there grudges, unforgiveness, or negative emotions within us? Self-examination helps us focus on the Lord rather than relying on our own efforts. It leads to the cultivation of the Fruits of the Holy Spirit in our lives.

Self-examination involves looking at our thoughts and self-talk, understanding what we say to ourselves daily. This process helps us identify harmful thoughts that may harm us and grieve the Holy Spirit. It's crucial to pray for God's guidance in self-examination, seeking understanding and wisdom from Him.

Asking God to search our hearts and lead us in the way everlasting (Psalm 139:23–24) is a powerful step. Opening our minds, ears, and eyes to God's Word and miracles, seeking understanding and guidance, and desiring to live in accordance with His will are essential aspects of this transformative journey. Let us commit to examining ourselves, seeking God's transformative power, and trusting in His guidance for a happier and more fulfilling life.

My story about God's constant presence and support started at Temple Baptist Church, where Pastor Pitman's preaching ignited a deep desire in me to immerse myself in the Word of God. Pastor Pitman is an amazing pastor, and we deeply appreciate his dedication to our congregation. He presents Bible lessons that meet our spiritual needs and officiates special occasions. His love for everyone and commitment to mission work are admirable.

Each Wednesday and twice on Sundays, Pastor's messages resonate with us, and I personally enjoy and love his preaching. His way of sharing God's Word is remarkable and understandable to all. His ongoing prayers, love, patience, and care are unmatched. His role has significantly impacted our spiritual journey, and we are sincerely thankful for his love and dedication.

Pastor's commitment to preaching the Word of God and being a great mentor is truly valued. He is a blessing to our community, and our love for him and our church has grown stronger over the thirty years we've been part of it. The preaching of the Word of God is vital to us, and Pastor's diligent studies encourage believers to deepen their relationship with the Lord.

Over the last thirty-five years, Pastor has brought many Godly speakers to the church. Temple Baptist School (TBS) also provides a wonderful atmosphere. My spiritual journey started with TBC's teachings and biblical events, leading me to transcribe the entire New Testament word by word. I've been reading and studying the entire Bible daily for over thirty years, with spiritual growth nurtured by various resources and attending numerous church services, revival meetings, and mission conferences.

The key to my understanding is asking God to open my mind as described in Luke 24:45. This has allowed me to grasp the scriptures deeply, serving God with a pure heart. It has also freed me from fears, worries, stress, and anxieties, as stated in John 14:27. My goal was to experience the freedom promised by God through Christ (Luke 4:18–19), and I am grateful that God heard my prayers (Psalm 34:6) and blessed me accordingly (Jeremiah 17:7). I have experienced firsthand that the word of God is alive and active, as emphasized in Hebrews 4:12. It is not a mere historical record or collection of inspirational thoughts; rather, it is the living and active power of God. The Word of God has penetrated my heart, soul, and spirit, providing a profound and transformative experience.

Trusting God means transferring your confidence and hope from yourself to Him. It's about knowing who God is more than what He will do and why. Imagine hanging from a rope in a deep well, and a voice tells you to let go. Trust is like that; it's a risk, but it's worthwhile because God is perfectly good and loving.

Children trust their parents for provision without worrying about the future. Similarly, we trust our heavenly Father to provide what we need each day.

Even when God's actions don't make sense, trust requires looking back at His past faithfulness. The psalmist encourages us to remember His miracles and deeds.

Trust leads to obedience. Only when we trust God can we desire and obey Him. Obedience is connected to abiding in Christ and bearing fruit.

Obedience is always worthwhile. While it may seem challenging, it's a learning process. God wants us to trust Him more than His methods. Trusting is about growing insight into who God is, not relying on specific outcomes.

God uses adversity to shape Christ-like character in us. He's more interested in changing us than our circumstances.

Dear family and friends, life can bring challenges that seem overwhelming, but it's crucial to realize that these are moments when God is trying to get our attention. It's like a signal for us to pause, reflect, seek God's wisdom, follow His Word, and trust Him for help (James 1:5 and Hebrews 4:16).

Facing difficulties exposes our weaknesses and encourages us to rely on God in ways we might not have considered. Even in trials, Jesus invites us to find rest in Him (Matthew 11:28–30). Adversity becomes a classroom where we learn more about Christ and grow to be more like Him.

I've personally learned obedience through facing adversities. In tough times, I found solace in God's Word and His presence. During unknown and challenging moments, I turned to God, seeking His strength to forgive and let go. Adversity became an opportunity to experience the good that God intended, turning darkness into light (Isaiah 42:16). I discovered strength in weakness, realizing that God's grace is always sufficient (2 Corinthians 12:7–10).

Adversity is like God's way of disciplining us for maturity, reminding us to fear the Lord and be accountable to Him (Proverbs 9:10, 14:27, 22:4). It encourages us to cry out to God, knowing He hears our prayers (Psalm 34:17). Adversity exposes pride, helps us hate sin, and prompts self-examination. It's a means through which God purifies our faith, strengthens us in spiritual warfare, and encourages us to reevaluate priorities.

In tough times, it's essential to examine if our work will last and if our friendships endure. It's an opportunity to experience God's power and prepare ourselves to comfort others with the comfort we receive from Him (2 Corinthians 1:3–5).

To get God's attention, we must strive to be clean before His eyes (James 4:17, 2 Timothy 2:15). This involves putting into practice what we know from His Word. Keeping His words demonstrates our love for Him, and He will walk with us through circumstances (John 14:15). Even when things seem difficult, we can find joy and strength in the Lord (Habakkuk 3:17–19).

Remember, in tough times, God is actively working in and through us. Trust Him, seek His guidance, and find comfort in His promises. He is always there for us, and we need to learn to seek Him instead of solely focusing on circumstances. Trust in the Lord with all your heart, lean not on your understanding, acknowledge Him in all your ways, and He will direct your paths (Proverbs 3:5–7).

Will you trust God in the darkness based on what He has revealed in the light?

Trust is seen in small things. Build trust in the little things in life and notice how God shows that He can be trusted in small decisions, which helps you trust Him in bigger ones.

To get better at trusting and obeying God, I have a daily routine where I ask Him for help. I ask for assistance in trusting Him, staying connected to the Lord, and following His Spirit throughout the day without quenching or grieving the Holy Spirit of God.

Here are some simple ways I've discovered to trust God completely:

1. I've learned to give all my worries and myself to God.
2. I've learned to replace negative thoughts with the teachings from the Word of God.
3. I've learned to ask God for patience.

4. I've learned to have confidence in what the Word of God says.
5. I've learned not to rely only on myself.
6. I've learned to be honest about my doubts.
7. I've learned not to hold onto worries because worrying is considered a sin.
8. I've learned to find truth in the scriptures.
9. I've learned to focus on things to be thankful for.
10. I've learned to trust in the Lord, both in good and bad times.

Throughout my life, the Holy Spirit has revealed various truths about God to me, primarily regarding trust, overcoming doubts, and battling unbelief.

These revelations have helped me love God with all my heart, and I hope they will also inspire and guide you.

1. *God is the truth:*
   - John 14:6—"Jesus saith unto him, I am the way, the truth, and the life: no man cometh unto the Father, but by me."
   - Deuteronomy 32:4—"He is the Rock, his work is perfect: for all his ways are judgment: a God of truth and without iniquity, just and right is he."
   - John 17:17—"Sanctify them through thy truth: thy word is truth."
2. *God is love:*
   - 1 John 4:8—"He that loveth not knoweth not God; for God is love."
3. *God is light:*
   - 1 John 1:5—"This then is the message which we have heard of him, and declare unto you, that God is light, and in him is no darkness at all."
4. *God is spirit:*
   - John 4:24—"God is a Spirit: and they that worship him must worship him in spirit and in truth."

- 2 Corinthians 3:17—"Now the Lord is that Spirit: and where the Spirit of the Lord is, there is liberty."

5. *God gives us new life:*
    - 2 Corinthians 5:17—"Therefore if any man be in Christ, he is a new creature: old things are passed away; behold, all things are become new."
6. *God gives us His Holy Spirit:*
    - Acts 1:8—"But ye shall receive power, after that the Holy Ghost is come upon you: and ye shall be witnesses unto me both in Jerusalem, and in all Judaea, and in Samaria, and unto the uttermost part of the earth."
    - Ephesians 1:13—"In whom ye also trusted, after that ye heard the word of truth, the gospel of your salvation: in whom also after that ye believed, ye were sealed with that holy Spirit of promise."
7. *God gives us victory over our issues:*
    - 1 John 5:4—"For whatsoever is born of God overcometh the world: and this is the victory that overcometh the world, even our faith."
8. *God gives us victory over satan:*
    - 1 John 4:4—"Ye are of God, little children, and have overcome them: because greater is he that is in you, than he that is in the world."
9. *God gives us peace:*
    - John 14:27—"Peace I leave with you, my peace I give unto you: not as the world giveth, give I unto you. Let not your heart be troubled, neither let it be afraid."
    - Psalm 119:165—"Great peace have they which love thy law: and nothing shall offend them."
    - Isaiah 26:3—"Thou wilt keep him in perfect peace, whose mind is stayed on thee: because he trusteth in thee."
10. *God gives us rest:*
    - Matthew 11:28–30— "Come unto me, all ye that labour and are heavy laden, and I will give you rest."

And much more…

In summary, my journey of faith and the guidance of the Holy Spirit have enabled me to discover these profound truths about God. These revelations have enriched my life and deepened my relationship with our Heavenly Father. I hope that these truths about God can also inspire and strengthen you on your spiritual journey.

Psalm 18:1–3 (KJV) says, "I will love thee, O LORD, my strength. The LORD is my rock, and my fortress, and my deliverer; my God, my strength, in whom I will trust; my buckler, and the horn of my salvation, and my high tower. I will call upon the LORD, who is worthy to be praised: so shall I be saved from mine enemies."

Understanding God's Desire to Know Us Personally

Understanding God's desire to know us personally is crucial for several reasons:

1. *Personal relationship.* Recognizing that God desires a personal relationship with us highlights the importance of connection and intimacy. It emphasizes that God isn't distant but seeks a close, personal bond with everyone.
2. *Unconditional love.* Knowing that God wants to know us personally reflects His unconditional love. It demonstrates that He values us individually, regardless of our flaws or mistakes.
3. *Purpose and meaning.* Understanding God's desire for a personal relationship gives a sense of purpose and meaning to our existence. It shows that our lives have significance to Him beyond mere existence.
4. *Guidance and direction.* Recognizing God's personal interest in us encourages seeking His guidance and direction in life. It prompts us to rely on His wisdom and support in decision-making.
5. *Comfort and support.* In times of trouble or loneliness, the understanding that God desires a personal relationship offers comfort and support. It provides solace in knowing that God is always there, eager to connect with us.

6. *Transformation.* God's desire to know us personally can lead to transformation and personal growth. It motivates us to align our lives with His will, fostering spiritual growth and character development.
7. *Identity and worth.* It reinforces our identity and worth as individuals created by God. Understanding His desire to know us personally affirms our value in His eyes.
8. *Eternal perspective.* Recognizing God's desire for a personal relationship extends beyond this life, offering an eternal perspective. It underscores the idea of an everlasting connection with God beyond the earthly realm.

In essence, understanding God's longing for a personal relationship helps establish a deep and meaningful connection with Him, shaping our spiritual journey and providing a sense of purpose, guidance, and assurance in our lives.

The power of personal relationship!

The most important question a person can ask is: Who is God? The God who created you has a purpose for your life. Life is God plus You. Deep inside your heart, you have a hope for greatness. You have a sense of eternity. You desire to love and be loved. You desire true peace, joy, and happiness. You desire eternal Life. These desires came from your Creator. You know that there must be more to life than in your current situation.

> The following verses from the Bible reveal God's longing for a close connection with us, reflecting His deep understanding and care for every person. They emphasize God's intimate knowledge and concern, showcasing His desire for a personal relationship with each individual, expressing His yearning for our friendship and closeness.

Thus says the LORD: "Let not the wise man glory in his wisdom, Let not the mighty man glory in his might, Nor let the rich man glory in his riches; But let him who glories glory in this, That he understands and knows Me, That I am the LORD, exercising lovingkindness, judgment, and righteousness in the earth. For in these I delight," says the LORD (Jeremiah 9:23–24 NKJV).

For it is God who commanded light to shine out of darkness, who has shone in our hearts to give the light of the knowledge of the glory of God in the face of Jesus Christ. (2 Corinthians 4:6 NKJV)

This revelation will increase until the earth is filled with the knowledge of the glory of God. For the earth will be filled with the knowledge of the glory of the LORD, As the waters cover the sea. (Habakkuk 2:14 NKJV)

And God spoke to Moses and said to him: "I am the LORD." I appeared to Abraham, to Isaac, and to Jacob, as God Almighty, but by My name LORD I was not known to them. (Exodus 6:2–3 NKJV)

Therefore say to the children of Israel: "I am the LORD; I will bring you out from under the burdens of the Egyptians, I will rescue you from their bondage, and I will redeem you with an outstretched arm and with great judgments. I will take you as My people, and I will be your God. Then you shall know that I am the LORD your God who brings you out from under the burdens of the Egyptians." (Exodus 6:6–7 NKJV)

To you it was shown that you might know that the LORD Himself is God; there is none other besides Him. Out of heaven He let you hear His voice, that He might instruct you; on earth He showed you His great fire, and you heard His words out of the midst of the fire. And because He loved your fathers, therefore He chose their descendants after them; and He brought you out of Egypt with His Presence, with His mighty power, driving out from before you, nations greater and mightier than you, to bring you in, to give you their land as an inheritance, as it is this day. Therefore, know this day, and consider it in your heart, that the LORD Himself is God in heaven above and on the earth beneath; there is no other. You shall therefore keep His statutes and His commandments which I command you today, that it may go well with you and with your children after you, and that you may prolong your days in the land which the LORD your God is giving you for all time. (Deuteronomy 4:35–40 NKJV)

The LORD did not set His love on you nor choose you because you were more in number than any other people, for you were the least of all peoples; but because the LORD loves you, and because He would keep the oath which He swore to your fathers, the LORD has brought you out with a mighty hand, and redeemed you from the house of bondage, from the hand of Pharaoh king of Egypt. Therefore, know that the LORD your God, He is God, the faithful God who keeps covenant and mercy for a thousand generations with those who love Him and keep His commandments; and He repays those who hate

Him to their face, to destroy them. He will not be slack with him who hates Him; He will repay him to his face. Therefore, you shall keep the commandment, the statutes, and the judgments which I command you today, to observe them. "Then it shall come to pass, because you listen to these judgments, and keep and do them, that the LORD your God will keep with you the covenant and the mercy which He swore to your fathers." (Deuteronomy 7:7–12 NKJV)

As for you, my son Solomon, know the God of your father, and serve Him with a loyal heart and with a willing mind; for the LORD searches all hearts and understands all the intent of the thoughts. If you seek Him, He will be found by you; but if you forsake Him, He will cast you off forever. (1 Chronicles 28:9 NKJV)

I know also, my God, that You test the heart and have pleasure in uprightness. As for me, in the uprightness of my heart I have willingly offered all these things; and now with joy I have seen Your people, who are present here to offer willingly to You. (1 Chronicles 29:17 NKJV)

How long, O you sons of men, Will you turn my glory to shame? How long will you love worthlessness And seek falsehood? Selah But know that the LORD has set apart for Himself him who is godly; The LORD will hear when I call to Him. (Psalms 4:2–3 NKJV)

The wicked in his proud countenance does not seek God; God is in none of his thoughts. (Psalms 10:4 NKJV)

I will instruct you and teach you in the way you should go; I will guide you with My eye. Do not be like the horse or like the mule, Which have no understanding, Which must be harnessed with bit and bridle, Else they will not come near you. Many sorrows shall be to the wicked; But he who trusts in the Lord, mercy shall surround him. (Psalms 32:8–10 NKJV)

Be still and know that I am God; I will be exalted among the nations, I will be exalted in the earth! The Lord of hosts is with us; The God of Jacob is our refuge. Selah. (Psalms 46:10–11 NKJV)

Serve the Lord with gladness; Come before His presence with singing. Know that the Lord, He is God; It is He who has made us, and not we ourselves; We are His people and the sheep of His pasture. Enter into His gates with thanksgiving, And into His courts with praise. Be thankful to Him and bless His name. For the Lord is good; His mercy is everlasting, And His truth endures to all generations. (Psalms 100:2–5 NKJV)

My son, if you receive my words, And treasure my commands within you, So that you incline your ear to wisdom, And apply your heart to understanding; Yes, if you cry out for discernment, And lift up your voice for understanding, If you seek her as silver, And search for her as for hidden treasures; Then you will understand the fear of the Lord, And find the knowledge of God. For the Lord gives wisdom; From His mouth come knowledge and understanding; He stores up sound wisdom for the upright; He is a shield to those who walk uprightly; He guards the paths of justice, And preserves the way of His saints. Then you will understand righteousness and justice, Equity and every good path. (Proverbs 2:1–9 NKJV)

"You are My witnesses," says the LORD, "And My servant whom I have chosen, That you may know and believe Me, And understand that I am He. Before Me there was no God formed, Nor shall there be after Me. I, even I, am the LORD, And besides Me there is no savior." (Isaiah 43:10–11 NKJV)

I am the LORD, and there is no other; There is no God besides Me. I will gird you, though you have not known Me, That they may know from the rising of the sun to its setting That there is none besides Me. I am the LORD, and there is no other. (Isaiah 45:5–6 NKJV)

Seek the LORD while He may be found, Call upon Him while He is near. Let the wicked forsake his way, And the unrighteous man his thoughts; Let him return to the LORD, And He will have mercy on him; And to our God, For He will abundantly pardon. (Isaiah 55:6–7 NKJV)

For I will set My eyes on them for good, and I will bring them back to this land; I will build them and not pull them down, and I will plant them and not pluck them up. Then I will give them a heart to know Me, that I am the LORD; and they shall be My people, and I will be their God, for they shall return to Me with their whole heart. (Jeremiah 24:6–7 NKJV)

Those who do wickedly against the covenant he shall corrupt with flattery; but the people who know their God shall be strong, and carry out great exploits. (Daniel 11:32 NKJV)

Hear the word of the LORD, You children of Israel, For the LORD brings a charge against the inhabitants of the land: "There is no truth or mercy Or knowledge of God in the land." (Hosea 4:1 NKJV)

My people are destroyed for lack of knowledge. Because you have rejected knowledge, I also will reject you from being priest for Me; Because you have forgotten the law of your God, I also will forget your children. (Hosea 4:6 NKJV)

They do not direct their deeds Toward turning to their God, For the spirit of harlotry is in their midst, And they do not know the LORD. (Hosea 5:4 NKJV)

Let us know, Let us pursue the knowledge of the LORD. His going forth is established as the morning; He will come to us like the rain, Like the latter and former rain to the earth. (Hosea 6:3 NKJV)

For I desire mercy and not sacrifice, And the knowledge of God more than burnt offerings. (Hosea 6:6 NKJV)

Israel will cry to Me, "My God, we know You!" Israel has rejected the good; The enemy will pursue him. (Hosea 8:2–3 NKJV)

Yet I am the LORD your God Ever since the land of Egypt, And you shall know no God but Me; For there is no savior besides Me. (Hosea 13:4 NKJV)

And this is eternal life, that they may know You, the only true God, and Jesus Christ whom You have sent. (John 17:3 NKJV)

And He has made from one blood every nation of men to dwell on all the face of the earth, and has determined their pre-appointed times and the boundaries of their dwellings, so that they should seek the Lord, in the hope that they might grope for Him and find Him, though He is not far from each one of us; for in Him we live and move and have our being, as also some of your own poets have said, 'For we are also His offspring. (Acts 17:26–28 NKJV)

And even as they did not like to retain God in their knowledge, God gave them over to a debased mind, to do those things which are not fitting. (Romans 1:28 NKJV)

Now we have received, not the spirit of the world, but the Spirit who is from God, that we might know the things that have been freely given to us by God. (1 Corinthians 2:12 NKJV)

But if anyone loves God, this one is known by Him. (1 Corinthians 8:3 NKJV)

Do not be deceived: "Evil company corrupts good habits." Awake to righteousness, and do not sin; for some do not have the knowledge of

God. I speak this to your shame. (1 Corinthians 15:33–34 NKJV)

Now thanks be to God who always leads us in triumph in Christ, and through us diffuses the fragrance of His knowledge in every place. (2 Corinthians 2:14 NKJV)

Nevertheless when one turns to the Lord, the veil is taken away. Now the Lord is the Spirit; and where the Spirit of the Lord is, there is liberty. But we all, with unveiled face, beholding as in a mirror the glory of the Lord, are being transformed into the same image from glory to glory, just as by the Spirit of the Lord. (2 Corinthians 3:16–18 NKJV)

For it is the God who commanded light to shine out of darkness, who has shone in our hearts to give the light of the knowledge of the glory of God in the face of Jesus Christ. (2 Corinthians 4:6 NKJV)

For the weapons of our warfare are not carnal but mighty in God for pulling down strongholds, casting down arguments and every high thing that exalts itself against the knowledge of God, bringing every thought into captivity to the obedience of Christ. (2 Corinthians 10:4–5 NKJV)

That the God of our Lord Jesus Christ, the Father of glory, may give to you the spirit of wisdom and revelation in the knowledge of Him. (Ephesians 1:17 NKJV)

That Christ may dwell in your hearts through faith; that you, being rooted and grounded in love, may be able to comprehend with all the saints what is the width and length and depth and height—to know the love of Christ which passes knowledge; that you may be filled with all the fullness of God. (Ephesians 3:17–19 NKJV)

Till we all come to the unity of the faith and of the knowledge of the Son of God, to a perfect man, to the measure of the stature of the fullness of Christ. (Ephesians 4:13 NKJV)

For this reason we also, since the day we heard it, do not cease to pray for you, and to ask that you may be filled with the knowledge of His will in all wisdom and spiritual understanding; that you may walk worthy of the Lord, fully pleasing Him, being fruitful in every good work and increasing in the knowledge of God; strengthened with all might, according to His glorious power, for all patience and longsuffering with joy; giving thanks to the Father who has qualified us to be partakers of the inheritance of the saints in the light. (Colossians 1:9–12 NKJV)

To them God willed to make known what are the riches of the glory of this mystery among the Gentiles: which is Christ in you, the hope of glory. (Colossians 1:27 NKJV)

That their hearts may be encouraged, being knit together in love, and attaining to all riches of the full assurance of understanding, to the knowledge of the mystery of God, both of the

Father and of Christ, in whom are hidden all the treasures of wisdom and knowledge. (Colossians 2:2–3 NKJV)

For this is the will of God, your sanctification: that you should abstain from sexual immorality; that each of you should know how to possess his own vessel in sanctification and honor, not in passion of lust, like the Gentiles who do not know God; that no one should take advantage of and defraud his brother in this matter, because the Lord is the avenger of all such, as we also forewarned you and testified. (1 Thessalonians 4:3–6 NKJV)

Grace and peace be multiplied to you in the knowledge of God and of Jesus our Lord, as His divine power has given to us all things that pertain to life and godliness, through the knowledge of Him who called us by glory and virtue, by which have been given to us exceedingly great and precious promises, that through these you may be partakers of the divine nature, having escaped the corruption that is in the world through lust. (2 Peter 1:2–4 NKJV)

Now by this we know that we know Him, if we keep His commandments. He who says, "I know Him," and does not keep His commandments, is a liar, and the truth is not in him. But whoever keeps His word, truly the love of God is perfected in him. By this we know that we are in Him. (1 John 2:3–5 NKJV)

Behold what manner of love the Father has bestowed on us, that we should be called children of God! Therefore, the world does not know us, because it did not know Him. Beloved, now we are children of God; and it has not yet been revealed what we shall be, but we know that when He is revealed, we shall be like Him, for we shall see Him as He is. And everyone who has this hope in Him purifies himself, just as He is pure. (1 John 3:1–3 NKJV)

We are of God. He who knows God hears us; he who is not of God does not hear us. By this we know the spirit of truth and the spirit of error. Beloved, let us love one another, for love is of God; and everyone who loves is born of God and knows God. He who does not love does not know God, for God is love. In this the love of God was manifested toward us, that God has sent His only begotten Son into the world, that we might live through Him. In this is love, not that we loved God, but that He loved us and sent His Son to be the propitiation for our sins. Beloved, if God so loved us, we also ought to love one another. No one has seen God at any time. If we love one another, God abides in us, and His love has been perfected in us. By this we know that we abide in Him, and He in us, because He has given us of His Spirit. (1 John 4:6–13 NKJV)

Understanding Essential Things about God!

Understanding essential things about God is crucial for several reasons:

1. *Relationship development.* Knowing fundamental truths about God helps in building a meaningful relationship with Him. Understanding His nature, character, and attributes forms the foundation of a personal connection.
2. *Guidance and direction.* Recognizing God's nature aids in seeking His guidance and direction in life's decisions. Knowing His principles helps in making choices aligned with His will.
3. *Faith strengthening.* A deeper understanding of God's nature strengthens faith. Knowing that He is trustworthy, just, loving, and omnipotent strengthens one's trust in Him during challenging times.
4. *Transformation.* Understanding God's attributes helps in personal transformation. His love, grace, and mercy inspire people to become more compassionate, forgiving, and merciful toward others.
5. *Worship and reverence.* Knowing essential truths about God enhances worship and reverence. Appreciating His holiness, sovereignty, and greatness fosters a deeper sense of awe and respect.

6. *Aid in teaching and sharing.* Having a clear understanding of God's nature facilitates teaching and sharing His message with others. It enables individuals to explain God's love and plan of salvation effectively.
7. *Peace and comfort.* Understanding that God is unchanging and faithful provides peace and comfort during turbulent times. It assures believers that God remains constant and reliable despite life's uncertainties.
8. *Purpose and meaning.* Knowing essential truths about God helps in understanding human purpose and existence. It provides a broader perspective on life's meaning and one's role in the world.
9. *Eternal perspective.* Knowing essential truths about God prepares individuals for eternity. Understanding His plan for salvation and the promise of eternal life brings hope and assurance beyond this earthly existence.
10. *Protection against false beliefs.* Understanding the truth about God acts as a shield against misconceptions and misleading teachings. It helps people discern between accurate, genuine beliefs and misleading or false information. When individuals have a clear understanding of God's nature, they can do the following:
    - *Identify truth.* Recognize teachings that align with the true nature of God. This discernment helps in distinguishing authentic spiritual guidance from misleading or erroneous teachings.
    - *Avoid deception.* Protect themselves from being misled by teachings that misrepresent God's character or intentions. Understanding God's true nature helps in filtering out misinformation or distorted beliefs.
    - *Strengthen faith.* Clarity about God's nature strengthens faith by providing a solid foundation based on truth. It helps in building a stronger, more resilient belief system that isn't easily swayed by false teachings.
    - *Develop discernment.* Enhance the ability to discern between genuine spiritual teachings and misleading

ideologies. This discernment empowers individuals to make informed choices about their spiritual beliefs and practices.

- *Cultivate stability.* Understanding the truth about God brings stability to one's beliefs and spiritual journey. It prevents confusion or doubt caused by contradictory or misleading information.
- *Promote unity.* When individuals share a common understanding of God's nature, it fosters unity within communities or groups. It prevents conflicts arising from misunderstandings or conflicting beliefs about God.
- *Encourage personal growth.* Clear understanding of God's nature encourages personal growth and maturity in faith. It promotes a deeper, more authentic relationship with God based on genuine understanding.
- *Uphold integrity.* It helps in maintaining integrity in one's spiritual beliefs and practices. Understanding God's truth prevents compromising beliefs based on misleading teachings.

In essence, understanding the truth about God acts as a safeguard, ensuring that individuals build their beliefs and practices on a solid and accurate foundation. This protects them from being led astray by teachings that misrepresent the nature and intentions of the divine.

God's Nature

- "God is spirit, and those who worship him must worship in spirit and truth" (John 4:24).
- "Anyone who does not love does not know God, because God is love" (1 John 4:8).
- "For in him all things were created: things in heaven and on earth, visible and invisible, whether thrones or powers or rul-

ers or authorities; all things have been created through him and for him" (Colossians 1:16).

God's Word

- "For the word of God is alive and active. Sharper than any double-edged sword, it penetrates even to dividing soul and spirit, joints and marrow; it judges the thoughts and attitudes of the heart" (Hebrews 4:12).

These verses provide a profound understanding of God's spiritual nature, His love, creative power, and the living and active nature of His Word. They offer a glimpse into the depth and majesty of God as revealed in the Scriptures.

Understanding the various aspects of God's character is fundamental to one's faith. Here are some important aspects of God's character based on biblical teachings:

1. *Love*
    - "Anyone who does not love does not know God, because God is love" (1 John 4:8).
    - "For God so loved the world, that he gave his only Son, that whoever believes in him should not perish but have eternal life" (John 3:16).
2. *Holiness*
    - "Exalt the Lord our God, and worship at his holy mountain; for the Lord our God is holy!" (Psalm 99:9).
    - "But just as he who called you is holy, so be holy in all you do; for it is written: 'Be holy, because I am holy'" (1 Peter 1:15–16).
3. *Mercy and compassion*
    - "But you, O Lord, are a God merciful and gracious, slow to anger and abounding in steadfast love and faithfulness" (Psalm 86:15).

- "The steadfast love of the Lord never ceases; his mercies never come to an end; they are new every morning; great is your faithfulness" (Lamentations 3:22–23).

4. *Justice*
    - "Righteousness and justice are the foundation of your throne; steadfast love and faithfulness go before you" (Psalm 89:14).
    - "For I the Lord love justice; I hate robbery and wrong..." (Isaiah 61:8).
5. *Faithfulness*
    - "Know therefore that the Lord your God is God, the faithful God who keeps covenant and steadfast love with those who love him and keep his commandments, to a thousand generations" (Deuteronomy 7:9).
    - "Your faithfulness endures to all generations; you have established the earth, and it stands fast" (Psalm 119:90).
6. *Wisdom*
    - "To the only wise God be glory forevermore through Jesus Christ! Amen" (Romans 16:27).
    - "Great is our Lord, and abundant in power; his understanding is beyond measure" (Psalm 147:5).
7. *Eternal and unchanging*
    - "Before the mountains were brought forth, or ever you had formed the earth and the world, from everlasting to everlasting you are God" (Psalm 90:2).
    - "Jesus Christ is the same yesterday and today and forever" (Hebrews 13:8).

These aspects provide a glimpse into the multifaceted nature of God as revealed in the Bible. Studying and meditating on these aspects can deepen one's understanding of the character of God.

Consider the following important aspects of God's character:

1. *God's love.* The unconditional love and compassion that God offers to humanity.
2. *Divine guidance.* How seeking God's guidance can provide direction and purpose in one's life.
3. *Faith and trust.* The role of our faith and our trust in one's relationship with God can provide strength during challenging times.
4. *Forgiveness and redemption.* The concept of forgiveness and the opportunity for redemption in the eyes of God.
5. *Divine plan.* The idea that God has a purpose and plan for each individual, even in the face of life's unexpected events.
6. *Miracles and providence.*
7. *Prayer and connection.* The significance of prayer as a means of connecting with God and seeking guidance.
8. *Moral and ethical values.* The role of God's teachings in shaping one's moral and ethical values.
9. *Personal relationship.* Anyone can cultivate a personal relationship with God and explore his/her spirituality.
10. *Hope and comfort.* Faith in God can provide hope, comfort, and a sense of purpose, especially in difficult times.

God is good, and you can trust Him with your life. "Oh, taste and see that the Lord is good; Blessed is the man who trusts in Him!" (Psalms 34:8).

God created the universe, including You; He is all powerful. "It is I who made the earth and created man upon it. I stretched out the heavens with My hands And I ordained all their host" (Isaiah 45:12).

God wants you to know Him, and know that He exercises loving-kindness, justice, and righteousness on earth. Thus says the Lord, "Let not a wise man boast of his wisdom, and let not the mighty man boast of his might, let not a rich man boast of his riches; but let him who boasts boast of this, that he understands and knows Me, that I am the Lord who exercises lovingkindness, justice and righteousness on earth; for I delight in these things," declares the LORD (Jeremiah 9:23–24).

God is holy, and He wants you to walk in holiness with Him. "But just as He who called you is holy, so be holy in all you do; for it is written: 'Be holy, because I am holy'" (1 Peter 1:15–16).

Dear family and friends, God wants you to be close to Him forever. He loves the world so much that He sent His only Son, Jesus, to save everyone who believes in Him from perishing but instead gives them eternal life (John 3:16–18).

Jesus tells us that to connect with God, to become His child, we must be born again, not physically but spiritually. This means having a new experience with God's love (John 3:3).

Being born again happens when you hear about Jesus and believe in Him. Believing in Jesus means trusting Him completely with your life. The good news is that Jesus came from God to save us from our mistakes and bring us back to God's family. He's the way to connect with God again. "I am the way, the truth, and the life. No one comes to the Father except through Me (John 14:6).

When Adam made a mistake, it brought sin and death to everyone (Romans 5:17). But Jesus offers us a way out. His name means "God rescues" or "God saves." Everyone who asks for help from the Lord will be saved. For whosoever shall call upon the name of the Lord shall be saved (Romans 10:13).

When you accept Jesus and believe in Him, you're receiving God's gift of grace. This is when you start living life with Jesus. It's like you were with Him when He died on the cross, and now your life is connected to His.

> In whom ye also trusted, after that ye heard the word of truth, the gospel of your salvation: in whom also after that ye believed, ye were sealed with that holy Spirit of promise. (Ephesians 1:13 KJV)

God didn't want robots; He wanted you to choose to love Him. He made you powerful with the freedom to choose. Jesus asks us to follow Him and be ready to give up our old ways to find a new life with Him. When you give your life to Christ by believing and trusting Him, it is counted that you were with Him on the cross, and your life is now joined to His life. *I am crucified with Christ: nevertheless, I live; yet not I, but Christ lives in me: and the life which I now live in the flesh I live by the faith of the Son of God, who loved me, and gave himself for me (Galatians 2:20).* Notice that you now live by the faith of Jesus, what He believes.

If you want to know God and give your life to Him, Jesus is the only way. No one else can save us. Jesus said He is the way, the truth, and the life. When you're born again, you become a follower of Jesus.

> There is salvation in no one else! For there is no other name under heaven given to mankind by whom we must be saved! (Acts 4:12 CJB)

Jesus taught that the most important thing is to love God with all your heart, soul, and mind. The second is to love others as you love yourself. All the rules hang on these two (Matthew 22:37–40).

God gives grace to those who are humble. If you want to be close to God, believe He exists and that He rewards those who look for Him with all their heart. But he gives us more grace. That is why Scripture says:

> God opposes the proud but gives grace to the humble." Submit yourselves, then, to God. Resist the devil, and he will flee from you. Come near to God, and he will come near to you. Wash your hands, you sinners, and purify your hearts, you double-minded. (James 4:6–8 NIV)

> But without faith, it is impossible to please Him, for he who comes to God must believe that He is, and that He is a rewarder of those who diligently seek Him. (Hebrews 11:6 NKJV)

Understanding the Love of God!

Understanding the love of God is crucial because it forms the foundation of our faith and shapes our relationship with Him. Here are some reasons why it's important to comprehend God's love:

1. *Identity and worth.* Recognizing God's love helps us understand our worth and identity. It affirms that we are valued and cherished by the Creator of the universe, regardless of our flaws or past mistakes.
2. *Connection and relationship.* God's love allows us to connect with Him on a personal level. Understanding His love enables us to build a deeper, more meaningful relationship with God, fostering intimacy and trust.
3. *Salvation and redemption.* God's love is displayed through the sacrifice of Jesus Christ, who died to save humanity from sin. Understanding this love leads to salvation and redemption, offering forgiveness and the opportunity for a renewed life.
4. *Transformation and growth.* Embracing God's love has the power to transform us. It motivates us to become better versions of ourselves, promoting positive change, growth, and the development of virtues like compassion, kindness, and forgiveness.
5. *Stability and assurance.* God's love provides stability and assurance in challenging times. Knowing that God loves us unconditionally gives us strength, hope, and peace, even amidst difficulties and uncertainties.

6. *Love for others.* Understanding God's love enables us to love others genuinely and selflessly. It inspires us to extend grace, forgiveness, and compassion to those around us, reflecting the same love that God has shown us.
7. *Purpose and fulfillment.* Recognizing God's love helps us understand our purpose. It motivates us to live a life that honors God, serve others, and find fulfillment in making a positive impact in the world.

Dear family and friends, understanding the love of God is essential because it shapes our identity, deepens our relationship with Him, leads to salvation, encourages personal growth, provides stability, motivates us to love others, and gives us a sense of purpose and fulfillment in life.

The word love is a central theme of the Bible and is mentioned over three hundred times in the King James version. The Bible speaks about the Creator's unconditional love for humankind, the love we ought to have for each other, and our love for God.

God's unconditional love or agape speaks to love that is pure and has no strings attached. Let's find out what the Bible has to say about unconditional love.

- What the Bible says about unconditional love?
    - o First John 4:8 KJV
    - o Song of Solomon 8:7 KJV
    - o 1 John 4:18 KJV
    - o 1 Peter 4:8 KJV
- Bible verses about God's unconditional love for me.
    - o Jeremiah 31:3 KJV
    - o Galatians 2:20 KJV
    - o Psalms 36:5–7 KJV
    - o Psalms 31:7 KJV
    - o Song of Solomon 2:4 KJV
- Bible verses about God's unconditional love for others.
    - o Romans 5:8 KJV
    - o Romans 8:35, 37 KJV

- Bible stories about God's unconditional love.
    - o The story of the Prodigal Son (Luke 15)
    - o Balaam (Numbers 22)
    - o Zacchaeus (Luke 19)

What the Bible says about unconditional love?

The Bible talks about unconditional love in various ways, often emphasizing the depth and breadth of love that's not contingent upon circumstances or actions.

1. *God's unconditional love.* One of the most famous mentions of unconditional love is in John 3:16: "For God so loved the world that he gave his one and only Son, that whoever believes in him shall not perish but have eternal life." This verse highlights God's love for humanity, demonstrating His willingness to sacrifice for humanity regardless of their actions.
2. *Love as a commandment.* In Matthew 22:37–39, Jesus summarizes the two greatest commandments: "Love the Lord your God with all your heart and with all your soul and with all your mind... Love your neighbor as yourself." This emphasizes a love that transcends conditions or requirements, advocating for a selfless and encompassing love for both God and others.
3. *Romans 8:38–39.* This passage describes how nothing—neither death nor life, angels nor demons—can separate believers from the love of God. It illustrates a love that endures despite any circumstances or challenges.
4. *First Corinthians 13.* Often referred to as the "Love Chapter," this passage details the characteristics of love, emphasizing its enduring nature, lack of envy or pride, and ability to endure all things. This portrayal suggests a love that operates independently of external factors.

These biblical references depict love as a love that is unconditional, steadfast, and selfless, extending beyond circumstances and expectations.

Love is this incredible feeling of closeness and affection we have for people—like friends, family, or even a higher power. It's this warm fondness we feel for others, caring about their well-being and showing kindness. Love can be seen in different ways: there's strong, passionate love between romantic partners, but there's also love guided by doing what's right, like caring for others even if you don't feel a strong attachment to them.

In the Bible, love is described in various ways. There's love guided by principles, like doing good things and caring for people even when it's tough. It's not just about feelings; it's about showing care and concern through actions. Different words are used for love in different contexts—like *agape*, which often means love based on doing what's right.

Love isn't just about feelings; it's also about actions. For instance, God's love is shown by giving His son, Jesus, as a gift to the world. Even if someone isn't feeling a strong affection, they can still show compassion and care, following the right principles.

But there's a difference between love based on doing what's right and love guided by self-interest. Loving someone because they love you back or because it benefits you isn't the same as genuinely caring for someone's well-being. Jesus encouraged loving even those who might be considered enemies, following the principle of love set by God, regardless of how you feel (Matthew 5:44).

The Bible talks about God being love itself. God is love (1 John 4:8). It's not that love is God, but rather that love is a core part of who God is. He shows love through creation and by caring for humanity. He's like a loving parent, doing everything possible for our well-being, even sacrificing His son out of love for us (John 3:16).

God's love isn't temporary—it's everlasting. It doesn't change based on our circumstances or actions. It's a constant, unwavering love that nothing can separate us from.

God's leadership is based on love. He wants people who choose to follow Him because they recognize His goodness and love rather than those seeking independence. This contrasts with those who reject His way because they think it's unfair or unloving.

Ultimately, love isn't just a feeling—it's about caring for others, doing what's right, and following principles set by a higher power, even when it's challenging.

God allowed tests and hardships, even leading to Jesus's death. God put Jesus through difficult times and trials to demonstrate His profound love. He stressed the importance of selflessly loving others, going as far as sacrificing oneself for friends. This new way of loving surpassed the older teachings about loving others just as you love yourself. God allowed tests and hardships and even permitted Jesus to endure death on the cross as a part of a larger plan. It was to fulfill the purpose of salvation for humanity. These trials were a testament to the depth of God's love for mankind, showcasing the extent to which He was willing to go to offer redemption and demonstrate His ultimate love and sacrifice.

This kind of love is cultivated through understanding God's teachings and spirit. Adam, though imperfect, passed on the capacity to love to future generations, but human love can often be misguided or twisted. True, godly love comes from seeking God's guidance and knowledge (1 Corinthians 13).

Love acts unselfishly, being patient, kind, and not envious. It doesn't boast or seek selfish gain. Love behaves respectfully and honorably, avoiding indecent or disruptive actions. Instead, it works toward the good of others, disciplines with kindness, and rejoices in truth and righteousness.

This love extends to loving God above all, loving fellow Christians, family, enemies, and even those who don't share the same beliefs. It's not confined or limited and doesn't seek its interests but focuses on what's good for others. This love, as shown through actions, is an essential quality for Christians to embody.

Love doesn't focus only on personal interests. It's about caring for others and their long-term well-being. It's shown by not always insisting on having things our way and being considerate of others' spiritual growth rather than demanding our own way or rights.

Real love doesn't easily get angry or look for reasons to be upset. It doesn't keep a record of wrongs done to us. Instead, it tries to understand and forgive, even when hurt.

Love isn't happy about dishonesty or injustice; it stands for truth, even if it challenges what we believed before. It prefers enduring harm to doing wrong to correct a situation. It's about speaking out for truth and fairness.

Love is patient and willing to cover over someone's mistakes if they ask for forgiveness and make amends. It's also about having faith in what God teaches, even if it seems hard to understand at times.

Love keeps hope alive, waiting for God's promises to come true, and it stays firm through challenges, especially when staying loyal to God is tested.

It's a powerful force that never fades away. However, it's not for those who reject God; there's a time to stop expressing love toward those who hate God.

Love in the Bible

1. *Different words for love.* The Bible talks about four types of love. The love emphasized here is "agape," which embodies selflessness and principle-based care rather than romantic attraction ("eros"), family-related affection ("storge"), or friendship ("philia").
2. *Nature of agape.* Agape isn't merely an emotion but a deliberate principle guiding our actions. It's the love that conquers natural inclinations and enables us to love even those we might not naturally like.
3. *Bible emphasis on love.* The Bible highly prioritizes this kind of love. Jesus highlighted it as the most important commandment, and Paul, in his writings, emphasized love's superiority over faith and hope.

Traits of Love (What It Is Not)

4. *Jealousy.* Love doesn't involve jealousy that causes rivalry or selfishness. While some forms of jealousy can have positive aspects, the jealousy associated with hate or resentment goes against love.
5. *Not boastful.* Love doesn't involve bragging or trying to show superiority over others. It humbly considers others' importance.
6. *Not proud.* Love is not haughty or self-important. It doesn't elevate itself above others but considers them as valuable.
7. *Not indecent.* Love doesn't behave rudely or offensively. It respects others' feelings and behaves with propriety.
8. *Not self-centered.* Love doesn't just look out for its own interests. It willingly gives preference to others' needs over its own.
9. *Not easily provoked.* Love doesn't quickly take offense or get irritated. It exercises self-control, especially in relationships.
10. *Doesn't keep score of wrongs.* Love doesn't hold grudges or keep track of wrongs done. It forgives and moves on after addressing the issue scripturally.
11. *Doesn't rejoice in wrongdoing.* Love doesn't find joy in unrighteousness or anything that goes against moral principles. It celebrates truth and righteousness.
12. *Never fails.* Love, based on God's nature, is enduring and reliable. It remains constant and capable in any situation.

Traits of Love (What It Is)

1. *Long-suffering.* Love is patient and willing to endure even when things are challenging or difficult.
2. *Kindness.* Love involves acts of kindness, thoughtfulness, and consideration for others' well-being.
3. *Rejoices with truth.* Love celebrates the triumph of truth and righteousness over falsehood.

4. *Bears all things.* Love covers over faults or mistakes of others and doesn't hold those against them.
5. *Believes all things.* Love is positive and trusting without being gullible or overly critical.
6. *Hopes all things.* Love is optimistic and hopeful about what God has promised in His Word.
7. *Endures all things.* Love perseveres and endures hardships without giving up.

"The Greatest of These Is Love"

> And now abideth faith, hope, charity, these three; but the greatest of these is charity. (1 Corinthians 13:13 KJV)

1. *The importance of love.*

Love is seen as the most crucial of human needs. A leading anthropologist compared it to the center of our needs, similar to how the sun is at the center of our solar system. Not being loved affects us physically and mentally. The Bible recognized this importance long ago.

2. *Different kinds of love.*

- *Romantic love.* Examples from the Bible show romantic love between couples like Isaac and Rebekah or Jacob's love for Rachel. However, it emphasizes the importance of this kind of love within the bounds of respect for God's principles.
- *Family love.* This kind of love is based on blood relations. An example is the deep affection between siblings Mary, Martha, and Lazarus.
- *Friendship love.* It's the affection between friends without romantic feelings. Examples are seen in the close bonds between David and Jonathan or Jesus and the apostle John.

- *Unselfish love (agape).* This type of love isn't just about emotions; it's selfless and focuses on doing good for others without expecting anything in return. This love, displayed by God in giving Jesus, is the highest form.

3. *Why love is greater than faith and hope.*

   - Love surpasses faith because even with great faith, without love, it's meaningless.
   - It's also greater than hope because hope often focuses on personal benefit and ends when the desired outcome is realized. Love, however, endures and never fails.

4. *Love as the greatest attribute of God.*

   - Love is considered the most significant of God's qualities because it motivates all that God does. God's love was the reason for creation, for providing redemption, and for offering the hope of an earthly paradise.

5. *Love as the foremost fruit of the Spirit.*

   - Love is listed as the first of the nine fruits of the spirit in the Bible. It's considered greater than joy, peace, long-suffering, kindness, goodness, faith, mildness, and self-control because it's the foundation that leads to and encompasses all the other qualities.

> But the fruit of the Spirit is love, joy, peace, longsuffering, gentleness, goodness, faith, Meekness, temperance: against such there is no law. (Galatians 5:22–23 KJV)

Why Love Is Greater Than Faith and Hope?

- *Love passes faith.*
- Paul says that love (agape) is greater than faith because even having immense faith or extraordinary abilities wouldn't matter if it's without love. If our pursuit of faith is selfish, it won't benefit us spiritually. Jesus pointed out that some might do powerful things but lack a genuine connection with him.
- *Love surpasses hope.*
- Agape love is greater than hope because hope can often be self-centered, focusing on personal gain. Love, however, isn't self-seeking. Hope, like the expectation of a better future, fades away once it's realized. Love, on the other hand, endures all things, never fading. It remains constant, unlike hope.

Greater Than Wisdom, Justice, and Power?

- *Love as God's primary attribute.*

  Love stands out as the foremost of God's attributes. God is described as love itself (1 John 4:8), and it motivates everything He does. God is never described in the scriptures as wisdom, justice, or power; these are qualities He possesses. Love is the driving force behind God's actions.
- *What drove God's creation.*

  Love prompted God to create the universe and beings like us. It wasn't merely wisdom or power; it was the desire to share joy with others. God's love found a way to remedy human faults caused by Adam's mistake. Love moved God to plan a paradise for obedient mankind.

Greatest of the Fruits of the Spirit

- *Love as the highest quality.*
  Love is placed above all other qualities of the spirit. It's ranked above joy, peace, and other virtues. Without love, joy is fleeting, peace is elusive, and other virtues are incomplete. Love is the foundation and brings about these qualities because God is love (1 John 4:8).
- *Examples of love's significance.*
  Love is like the backbone of lasting relationships and brings peace. It helps us be patient and kind to others. It's so important that it forms the base for all other good qualities, making it the most important among the fruits of the spirit.
- *Scriptural evidence for love's superiority.*
  Scriptures emphasize that loving others fulfills God's law. Even Jesus highlighted the importance of love for God and neighbors above all other commandments (Luke 10:27).

The Power of Love in a Christian's Life

- *What's most important?*
  Christians focus on many qualities to be effective, like knowledge, faith, hope, endurance, and self-control. But among these, love is the key. Without love, all other qualities lose their value. Love is central to everything.
- *Why love matters?*
  Love is like the paint that makes our lives colorful. It's what keeps us close and helps us understand and care about others. Love makes us want to help people and build connections. It's what inspires us to be kind, make sacrifices, and lend a hand. Love gives us comfort when we're feeling low, helps us heal, and makes us feel like we belong. Most importantly, it's what makes our world a better and more beautiful place.

Love matters to God because it embodies the very essence of His nature. God's love is unconditional, selfless, and boundless. It's the foundation of His relationship with humanity, driving His actions, guidance, and care for us. Through love, God expresses His desire for a deep and personal connection with each individual, seeking to bring them closer to Him. Love is the catalyst for forgiveness, redemption, and grace in God's plan for humanity, showing us the path to spiritual growth and fulfillment. Ultimately, love matters to God because it reflects His character and serves as the cornerstone of His relationship with us.

- *The significance of love.*
  Love isn't just about feelings; it's a powerful bond that surpasses selfishness. It's the motivation behind our actions. Loving others, as Jesus commanded, reflects our friendship with him and imitates God's nature.
- *Love balances everything.*
  While knowledge is essential, love ensures it doesn't make us prideful. Love tempers our desire for recognition or power. It keeps us humble and selfless. Balancing knowledge with love prevents arrogance.
- *Focusing on important priorities.*
  Love helps us prioritize. It's not about seeking position or recognition within the congregation but about genuinely caring for others. Pastors motivated by love benefit the congregation more than those seeking power.
- *Endurance through love.*
  Love helps us endure trials and hardships. Focusing solely on future rewards might lead to impatience or dissatisfaction when things get tough. Love makes us content, patiently waiting for God's promises, and keeps us selflessly serving others.
- *Whom should Christians Love?*
  Jesus taught us to love the Lord and our neighbors. Loving God develops over time as we learn about His kindness,

care, and actions toward us. As our knowledge of Him grows, our love deepens.

- *How do we show our love?*
  Loving God is shown through obedience to His Word and serving others. It's not just saying we love God but living according to His principles. Acts of kindness, honesty, and spreading the message of God's Kingdom reflect genuine love for Him.
- *The example of Jesus's love.*
  Jesus's life is the ultimate example of love. His self-sacrifice and compassion serve as a guide for us. Learning about his life and imitating his actions strengthen our love for him.
- *Cultivating love for Jesus.*
  Reading about Jesus in the Bible and understanding his sacrifices deepens our love for Him. This love is displayed through faith in Him and by emulating His selflessness. Remembrance of Jesus's sacrifice reinforces our appreciation for his love.

"Keep Loving Others"

Why is it good to imitate God's love?

Happiness comes from giving love, not just getting it. Jesus said it's better to give than receive (Acts 20:35). Our Heavenly Father shows us the ultimate love example. He's super loving and happy because of it! That's why imitating God by showing love makes us happy too. When we love like God does, we're not only happier, but we also please Him. He wants us to love each other (Romans 13:8).

Why Love Matters

Why is it vital to love fellow believers?

Loving others is the core of true Christianity. Jesus said to love one another just like he loved us (John 13:34–35). His love was self-sacrificing, putting others first. Our love should be just like that, even visible to people outside our group. It's what shows we're real followers of Christ.

What happens when love is missing?

Without love, everything else we do is pointless (1 Corinthians 13:1–2). Love is crucial in how we treat others, not just how much we love God or He loves us. Paul talks about what love looks like and what it's not.

What Love Looks Like

What does love involve?

Love means being patient and kind (Colossians 3:13). It's about showing kindness and truth, even when it's tough (Zechariah 8:16). Love also covers mistakes and believes the best about others (1 Peter 4:8). It endures tough times without giving up (Psalm 119:165).

What Love Isn't

What should love avoid?

Love isn't jealousy or bragging. It's not about showing off or behaving badly (Ephesians 5:3–4). Love isn't stubborn or quick to get upset (Ephesians 4:26). It doesn't keep a record of mistakes. Also, love doesn't find joy in someone else's mistakes but helps them get back on track (Proverbs 17:5).

"A Love That Lasts"

Why is love so special?

Why It's Vital to Love God

Back in Jesus's time, people debated which of the many laws was the most important. Some thought it might be about sacrifices or circumcision while others believed that lifting one law above others was wrong. To test Jesus, a Pharisee asked which commandment was the greatest. Jesus said, "Love the Lord your God with all your heart, soul, and mind." He added, "Love your neighbor as yourself." He said these two commands sum up true worship (Mark 12:28–34).

The Big Deal about Love

The Pharisees knew love for God was crucial, but many failed to show it. He understood that loving God meant more to Him than sacrifices. Think of it like this: a small gift given with lots of love means more to God than a huge one given without feeling. Jesus observed a poor widow give two small coins, and that meant a lot to God because it was given with genuine love.

How We Show Our Love

Love for God isn't just about feelings; it's about actions. We show our love for God by doing things that please Him, standing up for what's right, and obeying His rules. Just like how Jesus obeyed God, even sacrificing his life, we show our love by being obedient too.

Why We Should Love God

It makes sense to love God because He's shown us love first. God wants us to love Him because He cares for us deeply. He's like a loving parent who does everything for us and, in return, wants us to appreciate and love Him back.

Growing Our Love for God

We can't physically see God, but we can see Jesus, and we can build a loving relationship with Him. Learning about Jesus through the Bible helps us grow closer to Him. Also, reflecting on Jesus's life helps us understand God's love better. Plus, thinking about the amazing things God has given us makes us appreciate Him more.

The Good Stuff about Loving God

Meditating on the ways God has blessed us and His promises for the future helps us see how much He loves us. God listens to our prayers and has amazing plans for a world without suffering.

Friendship as Jesus Taught

Friendship, according to Jesus, is the greatest kind of love. He said this because real love is shown when someone is ready to give up their life for their friends. While many people think that romantic relationships and family are the most important types of love, Jesus taught that selfless love for friends is the most significant.

Jesus and Friendship

In the Bible, we see Jesus having deep friendships with people like Mary, Martha, Lazarus, and others. He showed affection to them and had meaningful connections, proving that friendships are essential.

Friendship and Family

Jesus believed in a chosen family through faith in Him. It's like picking friends but chosen by Jesus. This chosen family should love, forgive, and support each other just as real friends do. Jesus valued this kind of friendship even more than natural family ties.

Loving Others, including Enemies

Jesus taught us to be friendly even with people who don't share our beliefs. We should be a positive example and love others despite our differences. He even told a story where enemies showed love, emphasizing the importance of loving everyone.

Being Friends like Jesus

Our friendships with people shouldn't just be about trying to change them. Jesus made friends with people before they believed in Him. As His followers, we can be friends with people who believe like us and those who don't while still wanting the best for them.

No Greater Love

Jesus showed the greatest love by sacrificing His life for His friends. He demonstrated that loving friends selflessly is the highest form of love among people. This kind of love is different from the conditional love we often see, as Jesus showed love even to those who opposed Him.

These Bible verses also talk about friendship and love:

- "A friend loves at all times, and a brother is born for adversity" (Proverbs 17:17).
- "Greater love has no one than this: to lay down one's life for one's friends" (John 15:13).
- "A man of many companions may come to ruin, but there is a friend who sticks closer than a brother" (Proverbs 18:24).
- "If either of them falls down, one can help the other up. But pity anyone who falls and has no one to help them up" (Ecclesiastes 4:10)

These verses highlight the value and importance of friendship and love, according to the Bible.

Love Is More Important Than Anything Else
First Corinthians 13:1–13

The Bible talks about love and how it's much more important than some things people highly value, like speaking different languages, making predictions, understanding secrets, showing off knowledge, having strong faith, giving things to the poor, and or even being willing to die for what they believe in. Without love, all these things don't really matter!

Even if I can speak really well and persuade people, if there's no love, my words mean nothing. If I give everything, I have to help the poor but don't have love, it doesn't really count; it's just to feel less guilty. Even if I sacrifice a lot for being a Christian, without love, it's pointless. Love matters most because it lasts forever!

Love never fades away, unlike these other things. Speaking different languages and predicting the future will stop being important. Even all the knowledge people gain will become outdated. When everything is perfect or when people mature spiritually, these special abilities will fade away.

The Bible says these things will end, but faith, hope, and love will last forever. Love is the greatest because "God is love."

Now let's talk about what love means (1 Corinthians 13:4–13).

1. *Patience.* Love is patient, meaning it can wait and doesn't rush to act. It waits for the right time to help.
2. *Kindness.* Love is kind and helps others whenever it can.
3. *Not jealous or envious.* Love is generous and doesn't feel jealous of others' success.
4. *No boasting or bragging.* Love is humble and doesn't show off.
5. *Not proud.* Love is honest about its strengths and weaknesses, not showing off.
6. *Not rude.* Love is courteous and polite in how it behaves with others.
7. *Not selfish.* Love thinks of others before itself and doesn't just look out for its own interests.

8. *Not easily angered.* Love remains calm and doesn't get angry quickly.
9. *Forgiving.* Love forgives easily and doesn't keep a record of wrongs.
10. *Rejoicing in truth.* Love is honest and doesn't celebrate when bad things happen but celebrates when things are right.
11. *Protective.* Love always protects and keeps others safe.
12. *Trusting.* Love trusts others and believes in their good intentions.
13. *Hopeful.* Love hopes for the best in people and situations.
14. *Persevering.* Love keeps on going, always doing what's right and good.
15. *Never fails.* Love never stops being important. It always influences and satisfies people who have it because God is love, and God never ends.

Making Our Choice

Choosing to love God and stick close to Him brings life and blessings. So will you choose to love God and let that love keep growing? The choice is yours. Loving God is a way to a fulfilling and blessed life.

Understanding and Discovering the Nature of God!

Understanding the nature of God holds significant importance for several reasons:

1. *Foundation of faith.* Knowledge of God's nature forms the foundation of faith. It helps believers comprehend who God is, His attributes, and His character, providing a basis for trust and belief in His existence and promises.
2. *Relationship with God.* Knowing God's nature deepens the relationship with Him. Understanding His qualities, such as love, mercy, justice, and wisdom, allows for a more intimate and meaningful connection with the divine.
3. *Guidance and direction.* Awareness of God's nature guides believers in making decisions aligned with His will. Knowledge of His moral attributes and principles helps individuals discern right from wrong, leading to a more righteous and purposeful life.
4. *Prayer and worship.* Understanding God's nature enhances prayer and worship. It allows believers to approach God with reverence, gratitude, and humility, acknowledging His sovereignty and attributes while communicating with Him.
5. *Strengthening against false teachings.* Knowledge of God's nature protects against misconceptions and false teachings

about Him. It provides discernment to distinguish between accurate teachings and distorted beliefs about the Divine.

6. *Comfort and trust.* In challenging times, understanding God's nature provides comfort and fosters trust. Knowing that God is loving, compassionate, and faithful gives reassurance and peace amid difficulties and trials.
7. *Transformation and growth.* Awareness of God's nature encourages personal growth and transformation. As individuals strive to reflect His attributes in their lives, they develop virtues such as love, kindness, and forgiveness, contributing to spiritual maturity.
8. *Evangelism and sharing the faith.* Understanding God's nature enables believers to articulate their faith more effectively. It equips them to share the Good News and explain the character of God to others, inviting them into a relationship with Him.

Overall, understanding the nature of God is essential because it forms the basis of faith, deepens the relationship with Him, guides decisions, enhances worship, guards against falsehoods, offers comfort, fosters growth, and equips believers to share their faith with others.

God's humility is remarkable. He, the most important, lowered Himself to be with us. Jesus, despite His significance, came to Earth and sacrificed Himself to save us from our errors. His humility was huge; the greatest willingly took the least important place on the cross. Now, He urges us to live humbly.

Pride, thinking too highly of ourselves, goes against God's desires. C.S. Lewis described pride as an "anti-God state of mind." It's destructive, causing Adam and Eve to leave paradise and turning angels into devils. It's a significant issue for everyone. So embracing humility is crucial in drawing close to God.

Pride makes us pretend to be better than we are, hiding our faults. It's like making a false impression, trying to appear superior. But humility is about honesty. As Christians, impressing anyone but God isn't necessary. It might feel daunting, but it's right. God values the humble; He hears, likes, and helps them. Pride, however, displeases Him.

Humility means being truthful with God and ourselves. When we confess our mistakes, God forgives us. It's better to be honest and humble than to pretend.

Understanding our place compared to God's is vital. He is incredible and holy while we are not. Humility is grasping this truth. Pride involves comparisons and thinking we're better than others, which upsets God. He wants us to be humble and acknowledge who we truly are.

We're cherished by God because of His love. Jesus forgives us and offers us a fresh start. This truth is humbling and beautiful.

Humility is the path to gaining God's attention. Bowing down before Him in humility draws us closer to Him.

God's Nature

The Bible describes God as the All-Powerful Creator of the universe, existing in three divine persons—Father, Son, and Holy Spirit. He is holy, loving, perfect, trustworthy, and our ultimate salvation.

Selected Bible Verses

1. "God is light, and in Him, there is no darkness" (John 4:24)
2. "Meditate on God's word day and night for success and courage, knowing God is always with you" (Joshua 1:8–9).
3. "Behold, God is my helper; the Lord upholds my soul" (Psalm 54:4)
4. "Who is like you, O Lord, majestic in holiness, doing wonders?" (Exodus 15:11)
5. "See what great love the Father has lavished on us, that we should be called children of God!" (1 John 3:1)

Attributes of God

- All-Knowing, Holy, Righteous, Just, Faithful, Wise, Eternal, Unchanging, Love.

God in the Old Testament

The God revealed in the Old Testament is the same in the New Testament, pointing to our need for a Messiah, fulfilled in Jesus Christ.

God revealed in Jesus Christ

Jesus, the Second Person of the Trinity, is God Himself. He came to redeem and reconcile humanity through His sacrifice.

God is love

God's love is demonstrated in sending His Son for the salvation of humanity.

God's ultimate goal

God's plan is one of love, redemption, and glorification for those who seek Him.

Finding God

God is knowable, close, and desires a personal relationship with those who seek Him.

What God says about Himself

I am who I am. (Exodus 3:14)

> The Lord, compassionate and gracious, slow to anger, abounding in love and faithfulness. (Exodus 34:6)

> I have not spoken in secret; I speak the truth and declare what is right. (Isaiah 45:19)

According to the Bible, God is described as the supreme and infinite Creator of the universe, the one true and living God who reveals Himself to humanity.

Here's a comprehensive understanding of who God is according to the Bible:

1. *Monotheistic.* The Bible declares the monotheistic nature of God, affirming that there is only one God. This is evident in verses like Deuteronomy 6:4, which states, "Hear, O Israel: The LORD our God, the LORD is one."
2. *Eternal.* God is eternal, existing from everlasting to everlasting. Psalm 90:2 expresses this attribute, saying, "Before the mountains were brought forth, or ever you had formed the earth and the world, from everlasting to everlasting you are God."
3. *Omnipotent.* God is all-powerful. He has the ability to do anything that is consistent with His nature and character. Revelation 19:6 proclaims, "For the Lord our God the Almighty reigns.
4. *Omniscient.* God is all-knowing. He has complete knowledge of everything, including the past, present, and future. Psalm 147:5 states, "Great is our Lord, and abundant in power; his understanding is beyond measure."
5. *Omnipresent.* God is present everywhere. He is not limited by time or space. Jeremiah 23:23–24 affirms this, saying, "Am I a God at hand, declares the LORD, and not a God far away? Can a man hide himself in secret places so that I cannot see him? Declares the LORD. Do I not fill heaven and earth? Declares the LORD."

6. *Immutable.* God is unchanging. He remains the same in His character, purposes, and promises. Malachi 3:6 declares, "For I the LORD do not change."
7. *Holy.* God is perfectly pure and separate from sin. His holiness is emphasized throughout the Bible, and Isaiah 6:3 illustrates it, saying, "Holy, holy, holy is the LORD of hosts; the whole earth is full of his glory!"
8. *Loving and merciful.* The Bible portrays God as loving and merciful. He extends grace, compassion, and forgiveness to humanity. John 3:16 affirms, "For God so loved the world, that he gave his only Son."
9. *Just and righteous.* God is perfectly just and righteous. He judges with fairness and equity. Psalm 89:14 declares, "Righteousness and justice are the foundation of your throne; steadfast love and faithfulness go before you."
10. *Trinitarian nature.* The New Testament reveals a Trinitarian understanding of God, comprising God the Father, God the Son (Jesus Christ), and God the Holy Spirit. They are distinct yet coeternal and coequal.
11. *Creator.* God is the Creator of the heavens and the earth. Genesis 1:1 famously states, "In the beginning, God created the heavens and the earth."
12. *Redeemer.* God is also portrayed as the Redeemer of humanity, offering salvation through Jesus Christ. John 3:17 expresses this, saying, "For God did not send his Son into the world to condemn the world, but in order that the world might be saved through him."
13. *Covenant-Maker.* Throughout the Bible, God establishes covenants with His people, outlining His promises and expectations for them. The Abrahamic, Mosaic, and New Covenants are prominent examples.
14. *Personal.* God desires a personal relationship with humanity. He communicates with individuals and desires their worship and obedience. Matthew 6:9 illustrates this in the Lord's Prayer, "Our Father in heaven."

Understanding who God is according to the Bible provides a foundational perspective for us believers and a framework for our faith and relationship with Him. It encompasses attributes of holiness, love, justice, and grace, revealing a God who is both transcendent and immanent.

> For the invisible things of him from the creation of the world are clearly seen, being understood by the things that are made, even his eternal power and Godhead; so that they are without excuse. (Romans 1:20 KJV)

If you are honest with yourself and believe that there is a Creator God, the next question is, Who is God? There are things that we can learn about the Creator from the creation. The Creator must have a purpose for the creation. There is one Creation that stands out above all others: people. God must have a purpose for designing and creating you. Deep inside, you have a desire to know the purpose for your life.

Each person seeks a "life philosophy" or a "religion." It starts with believing or disbelieving in God. This philosophy shapes our decisions, guiding us on what's right and wrong. It's a natural part of who we are.

We're designed to communicate. Considering how communication affects our world, it's logical that the Creator is a communicator too. If He made us for a purpose, He would reveal it to us. It's likely that the Creator makes Himself known so we can understand our purpose.

Various religions attempt to explain and connect with God. But Christianity stands apart. While others stress doing or becoming something to be accepted by God, Christianity offers salvation as a free gift. This God, a God of love, offers to change us and bring us closer to Him through Jesus Christ. His invitation is for everyone burdened by life's troubles.

The Bible, history's most influential book, claims to reveal God and our purpose. It accurately depicts our past, present, and future.

Its historical accuracy and predictions have made it widely believed across nations and cultures.

God's communication is clear through Jesus Christ and the Bible, as well as the countless lives transformed by Jesus. The Gospel has spread globally for centuries.

Despite being the most persecuted religion, Christianity continues to spread. Believers face threats, imprisonment, and even death. Yet many consider Jesus worth living and dying for.

God desires a relationship with us. It's astounding that the Creator desires our love. He made us valuable to Him. He sent His Son not to condemn but to save the world. Believing in Him brings eternal life.

God's love for us is evident in the Bible. His desire is for us to come into the light, away from darkness and wrongdoing.

Understanding the Truth about God Gives Us Peace

Knowing the truth about God can indeed bring a deep sense of peace, as emphasized in the Bible. Here's how this connection between knowing the truth about God and experiencing peace is explained according to the Scriptures:

1. *Understanding God's character.* When you come to know the truth about God's character as revealed in the Bible—His love, mercy, faithfulness, and sovereignty—you can find peace in His unchanging nature. Knowing that God is a loving and caring Father who is in control of all things can bring a sense of security and peace (Psalm 136:26; Lamentations 3:22–23).
2. *Assurance of salvation.* Knowing the truth about God's plan for salvation through Jesus Christ can bring profound peace. When you understand that through faith in Jesus, your sins are forgiven, and you have eternal life, you can experience peace of mind (John 3:16; Romans 5:1).
3. *Freedom from fear.* Knowing the truth about God's promise to be with you and to protect you can alleviate fear and anxiety. God's presence and care provide a sense of security and peace in the face of life's challenges (Isaiah 41:10; Philippians 4:6–7).
4. *Guidance and direction.* Recognizing that God is a source of wisdom and guidance can lead to a sense of peace in mak-

ing life's decisions. Proverbs 3:5–6 encourages trust in the Lord, and when you acknowledge Him in all your ways, He will direct your paths.

5. *Contentment.* Knowing the truth about God's provision and sovereignty can lead to contentment. Believing that God will supply your needs and that His plan is perfect can bring peace and a sense of acceptance (Philippians 4:19; Romans 8:28).
6. *Rest for the soul.* Jesus invites those who are weary to come to Him for rest (Matthew 11:28). When you come to know the truth about Jesus and His offer of rest for your soul, you can find inner peace and rest from life's burdens.
7. *Freedom from condemnation.* Knowing the truth about God's forgiveness and grace can bring freedom from guilt and condemnation. Romans 8:1 declares, "There is therefore now no condemnation for those who are in Christ Jesus."
8. *Hope in trials.* The Bible encourages believers to consider trials as opportunities for growth and refinement. Knowing the truth about God's faithfulness in the midst of difficulties can lead to a sense of peace and hope (James 1:2–4; Romans 8:28).
9. *Reconciliation with God.* Knowing the truth about God's desire for reconciliation through Christ allows you to have peace in your relationship with God. Second Corinthians 5:18 states, "All this is from God, who through Christ reconciled us to himself."
10. *Eternal perspective.* Understanding the truth about the eternal hope and promises of God can provide a sense of peace in the face of life's uncertainties. The Bible speaks of a future with God in His presence, free from suffering and sorrow (Revelation 21:3–4).
11. *Sense of purpose.* Understanding and believing in God's truth can give us a profound sense of purpose in life. It can provide a framework for our existence, answering questions about the meaning and direction of our lives. This clarity

of purpose can bring inner peace as it helps us feel our lives have significance.

12. *Hope and trust.* Belief in God's truth can instill hope and trust in our heavenly Father. Knowing that there is a divine plan or purpose can provide a source of comfort and assurance, even in the face of adversity. This hope and trust can bring a sense of peace, as it reduces anxiety and fear about the unknown.
13. *Guidance.* It will be nice if we could turn to our faith and belief in God for guidance. This guidance can help us make ethical and moral decisions, which in turn can lead to a sense of peace because then we are living in alignment with right and truthful beliefs.
14. *Forgiveness and redemption.* Belief in God often includes the concept of forgiveness and redemption. Knowing that we can be forgiven for our past mistakes and knowing that we can experience spiritual renewal will bring peace by relieving guilt and offering a fresh start.
15. *Connection and support.* Believing in God can provide a sense of connection to a larger spiritual community, offering support, fellowship, and a sense of belonging. Knowing that others share similar beliefs can be comforting and reassuring, contributing to inner peace.
16. *Gratitude.* Understanding and acknowledging God's truth often leads to a sense of gratitude for the blessings in our lives. Gratitude is closely linked to feelings of contentment and peace.

Understanding the truth about God, as revealed in the Bible, brings peace, assurance, comfort, guidance, and hope in life's challenges.

The most critical aspect of seeking God is desiring truth. Truth is found in Jesus Christ, who declares Himself as the Way, the Truth, and the Life.

God's truth is unchanging. Seeking truth demands humility and rejecting personal pride. There are only two paths: God's way or one's way. God desires love through belief and trust in Him.

God's promises are unshakable, confirming His unchanging nature. Jesus Christ remains constant, unaltered by time or teachings.

Salvation involves repentance and faith in Jesus, receiving the Holy Spirit at that moment. The Holy Spirit transforms us, the greatest gift from God.

My heartfelt desire is to ensure that my family, friends, and others I know receive the truth and salvation. It is crucial to me that their names are recorded in the Book of Life (Revelation 20:12). Among all important matters, nothing compares to securing their salvation and having the Holy Spirit in their lives.

The victorious life is marked by peace, confidence, and joy in the Lord, leading to constant fellowship with Him. It means to triumph over all kinds of sins through the Holy Spirit's transformative power.

Here are just a few of the many benefits of having the Holy Spirit of God live in you:

Having the Holy Spirit of God living within a person is a central belief in the Bible.

Here are some of the benefits associated with the indwelling of the Holy Spirit:

1. *Guidance.* The Holy Spirit is the source of guidance and wisdom. All believers experience a sense of divine direction in their lives, helping them make choices that align with their faith and values.
2. *Comfort.* The Holy Spirit is often referred to as the Comforter. It can provide solace and reassurance during times of sorrow, grief, or difficulty, bringing a sense of peace and consolation.
3. *Conviction.* The Holy Spirit can convict individuals of their need for spiritual growth and transformation, leading to repentance and a desire to live in a manner that is pleasing to God.

4. *Empowerment.* The Holy Spirit empowers believers with spiritual gifts and abilities. This empowerment can enable believers to serve others, evangelize, and live a life of purpose.
5. *Fruit of the Spirit.* The Holy Spirit produces "The fruit of the Spirit" in the lives of believers, which includes qualities such as love, joy, peace, patience, kindness, goodness, faithfulness, gentleness, and self-control. These virtues can lead to more fulfilling and harmonious relationships.
6. *Intercession.* The Holy Spirit intercedes on behalf of believers, helping them in their prayers and bringing their needs and desires before God.
7. *Transformation.* The presence of the Holy Spirit leads to personal transformation, helping individuals become more Christ-like in character and conduct.
8. *Unity.* The Holy Spirit is a unifying force, bringing believers together in faith, fellowship, and common purpose.
9. *Assurance.* Believers may find assurance in their faith through the presence of the Holy Spirit, knowing that they are children of God and have eternal life.

Jesus spoke of the Holy Spirit as "He." Jesus said:

> He shall speak of me. (John 15:26)
>
> I will send Him unto you. (John 16:7)
>
> He shall glorify me. (John 16:14)
>
> He shall not speak of Himself. (John 16:13)

He does work in the hearts of all people everywhere. So everyone anywhere can get saved! That is an incredible power and benefit for us to realize and to have, for He can change the hearts and minds of everyone anywhere, including our loved ones abroad. Also, we can get the Holy Spirit to change us so we can be reconciled to one another. The Holy Spirit's presence within us enables us to understand and interpret God's Word. Jesus told His disciples that "when he, the Spirit of truth, comes, he will guide you into all truth" (John 16:13). He reveals to our minds the whole counsel of God, the entire Bible. He is the ultimate counselor and guide for our lives. He leads us in the way we should go in all spiritual things. Without such a counselor, we would fall into error. In summary, He will draw the unsaved to Jesus, will convict both saved and unsaved, will change us, will draw us closer to the Lord, will sanctify us in the Lord, will help us with our prayer life, will guide us into all truth, will teach us all things, will anoint us with His divine power, will be our helper and comforter in this life and will produce the fruits of the Spirit (love, joy, peace, long-suffering, gentleness, goodness, faith, meekness and temperance) in us if we do not grieve Him (Ephesians 4:30) nor quench Him (1 Thessalonians 5:19).

> Moreover, I will give you a new heart and put a new spirit within you; and I will remove the heart of stone from your flesh and give you a heart of flesh. I will put My Spirit within you and cause you to walk in My statutes, and you will be careful to observe My ordinances. (Ezekiel 36:26–27 KJV)

> Jesus answered, "Truly, truly, I say to you, unless one is born of water and the Spirit he cannot enter into the kingdom of God. That which is born of the flesh is flesh, and that which is born of the Spirit is spirit. Do not be amazed that I said to you, 'You must be born again.' The wind blows where it wishes and you hear the sound of it, but do not know where it comes from and where it is going; so is everyone who is born of the Spirit." (John 3:5–8 KJV)

> He saved us, not on the basis of deeds which we have done in righteousness, but according to His mercy, by the washing of regeneration and renewing by the Holy Spirit. (Titus 3:5 KJV)

Jesus's phrase "born of water and the Spirit" (John 3:5) harks back to Ezekiel 36:25–27, where God is pictured as symbolically cleansing persons from sin's pollution (by water) and bestowing a "new heart" by putting his Spirit within them.

For me, the knowledge that the Holy Spirit of God lives in our lives and that He will never leave us or forsake us is cause for great confidence, joy, peace, and comfort. I thank God for His precious gift—the Holy Spirit and His work in our lives! That's why I want my friends and family to have these blessings as well.

Understanding and Grasping the Concept of Sin

Understanding and grasping the concept of sin from the Bible is important for several reasons:

1. *Understanding right from wrong.* Sin defines what is morally right or wrong according to God's standards. It provides a framework for discerning ethical behavior and guides individuals in making righteous choices.
2. *Awareness of separation from God.* Sin, as depicted in the Bible, signifies a separation from God. Recognizing sin helps individuals understand the disruption in their relationship with the Divine caused by actions contrary to God's will.
3. *Acknowledging moral standards.* The concept of sin establishes moral standards and guidelines. It provides a framework to differentiate between right and wrong, offering a basis for ethical behavior and decision-making.
4. *Recognizing our imperfections.* Understanding sin helps individuals recognize their own imperfections and shortcomings. It acknowledges the universal human condition of falling short of God's perfect standards.
5. *Awareness of consequences.* Sin carries consequences, both spiritually and sometimes physically or emotionally. Knowing the consequences of sin helps individuals understand the impact of their actions and behavior.

6. *Importance of redemption.* Understanding sin highlights the need for redemption and salvation. It emphasizes the significance of God's grace and the redemptive work of Jesus Christ in offering forgiveness and reconciliation with God.
7. *Humility and repentance.* Grasping the concept of sin fosters humility and encourages repentance. It leads individuals to acknowledge their mistakes, seek forgiveness, and strive for personal and spiritual growth.
8. *Healthy relationships.* Understanding sin contributes to healthier relationships. It promotes empathy, forgiveness, and understanding in relationships by recognizing that all individuals are fallible and in need of grace.
9. *Respecting God's holiness.* Understanding sin helps individuals appreciate the holiness of God. It emphasizes the vast difference between humanity's fallen nature and God's perfect and righteous character.
10. *Avoiding self-righteousness.* Recognizing sin prevents self-righteousness and judgmental attitudes toward others. It encourages compassion and mercy toward those struggling with their own failings.
11. *Aiding in restoring relationships.* Recognizing sin helps in restoring broken relationships. It encourages seeking forgiveness and reconciliation with others, promoting harmony and peace in personal interactions.
12. *Guidance for spiritual life.* Understanding sin provides guidance for a righteous and meaningful spiritual life. It encourages individuals to align their actions with God's will, fostering a closer relationship with Him.
13. *Avoiding harmful consequences.* Awareness of sin helps individuals avoid harmful consequences. It serves as a warning against actions that can lead to personal, societal, or spiritual harm.
14. *Sharing the gospel.* Grasping the concept of sin enables believers to share the gospel effectively. It helps in explaining the need for salvation and the transformative power of God's love and grace.

In essence, understanding sin from the Bible is crucial as it forms the basis for moral guidance, humility, repentance, awareness of consequences, appreciation of redemption, spiritual growth, and fostering healthier relationships based on compassion and grace.

Each culture has its own interpretation of what it means to commit a sin. While sins are generally considered actions, any thought, word, or act considered immoral, selfish, shameful, harmful, or alienating might be termed sinful.

Sin is a riddle, a mystery, a reality. Sin includes a failure to do what is right. But sin also offends people; it is violence and lovelessness toward other people and, ultimately, rebellion against God.

According to the Bible, sin is often defined as a transgression of God's law or a deviation from His will. The concept of sin is fundamental in Christian theology and is found throughout the Old and New Testaments. Here are some key aspects of sin according to the Bible:

1. *Breaking God's commandments.* Sin is often associated with violating God's commandments, as outlined in the Old Testament, such as the Ten Commandments. These commandments provide a moral and ethical framework for human behavior.
2. *Missing the mark.* The word "sin" is derived from an archery term, which means "to miss the mark." In this context, sin is seen as falling short of God's perfect standard of righteousness.
3. *Original sin.* The concept of original sin refers to the inherent sinful nature passed down from Adam and Eve, the first human beings. This original sin is the root of all human sinfulness.
4. *Repentance.* The Bible emphasizes the importance of repentance, which is the acknowledgment of one's sins, a turning away from them, and seeking forgiveness from God. This is a key step in addressing and dealing with sin.
5. *Consequences.* The Bible teaches that sin has consequences, both in this life and in the afterlife. It can lead to spiri-

tual separation from God and bring about suffering and hardship.

6. *Forgiveness and redemption.* The Bible also emphasizes God's grace and the possibility of forgiveness and redemption. Through faith in Jesus Christ, many can be forgiven and reconciled with God, even in the presence of sin.
7. *Freedom from sin.* The New Testament teaches that believers can find freedom from the power of sin through the indwelling of the Holy Spirit and a transformed life in Christ.

Sin in the Bible is often viewed as a violation of God's moral and ethical standards and the need for repentance and redemption through faith.

Further, the Bible teaches that sin involves a condition in which the heart is corrupted and inclined toward evil. There is a truth about sin that we often don't want to admit—sin is destructive.

Sin destroys families. It destroys relationships. It destroys careers. It destroys ministries. If you allow it to linger, it will destroy everything in its path. This is why sin is so dangerous.

There are so many examples from the Bible that show the devastation that happens as a result of sin. However, you do not even have to open the Bible. Just look around at all the brokenness we see in our world. It is all the result of the devastating nature of sin.

One reason you must avoid sin is because it seeks to destroy you. Sin initially appears as good fruit, pleasing to the eye, but behind it are destructive consequences that seek to ruin your life.

> If we say we have no sin, we deceive ourselves, and the truth is not in us. If we confess our sins, he is faithful and just to forgive us our sins and to cleanse us from all unrighteousness. If we say we have not sinned, we make him a liar, and his word is not in us. (1 John 1:8–10)

The best way to define sin is to compare it with something much more familiar: viruses. Most of us have experienced a cold or the flu. Both are fairly minor, but viruses have caused large-scale outbreaks throughout history. We have seen examples of these even recently. Here are some examples:

- Human immunodeficiency virus (HIV) in 1981.
- Swine flu (H1N1) in 2009.
- COVID-19 in 2019.

Each of these outbreaks caused illness and death across multiple continents and people groups. Sin is similar in that you can also point to past outbreaks. The first one happened soon after the earth was formed. When God finished creating the world, He said it was "*very good*" (Genesis 1:31). There was no suffering, problems, or evil.

This was true until the first man (Adam) and woman (Eve) did not listen to (disobeyed) God. At that moment, sin arrived and sparked a pandemic of sin. The Bible says, "When Adam sinned, sin entered the world. Adam's sin brought death, so death spread to everyone, for everyone sinned" (Romans 5:12). This outbreak of sin (DNA) continues today, and it is the most serious challenge we face.

A virus infects a person by injecting parts of itself into our good cells. Then the virus reprograms those cells to make more of the virus. Sin is a spiritual virus that infects every part of our lives. Once it gets a foothold, it grows. Sin can affect us physically, but it makes us spiritually and morally weak. If left unchecked, it will invade your emotions, conscience, desires, and every other part of you. The Bible adds, "And when sin is allowed to grow, it gives birth to death" (James 1:15).

Perhaps the most serious aspect of sin is that it is the only thing that separates us from God.

> Behold, the Lord's hand is not shortened, that it cannot save; neither His ear heavy, that it cannot hear: But your iniquities have separated between you and your God, and your sins have

> hid His face from you, that he will not hear.
> (Isaiah 59:1–2)

Because God is holy, sin cannot dwell in his presence. Thus, it is the reason why it separates us from him. Romans 8 talks about what can separate us from the love of God. The argument Paul was making is that there is nothing and no one that could ever separate us from God's love. Nothing that happens to us or is done to us will ever keep us from God's love. However, while nothing outside of us can separate us from God's love, the choices we make can. Meaning that if we choose to live in sin and continue in sin, we will ultimately be separated from God's love. Remember, God is holy.

According to the Bible, sin is defined as the breaking or transgression of God's law, disobedience or rebellion against God, and independence from God. Sin had its beginning with Lucifer, who desired to be higher than God (Isaiah 14:12–14) and brought sin to humanity in the garden of Eden. Sin is any action, feeling, or thought that goes against God's standards, including breaking God's laws and failing to do what is right. The Christian definition of sin is purposely disobeying the rules of God.

What Is Biblical Sin?

Learning from human history facts from the Bible, *three sins lie behind discontentment: pride, rebellion, and unbelief.* These are the original sins of the devil and his angels. They are sins that come from hell itself, and they continue in hell forever.

1. Discontent is a manifestation of pride.

These people always complain and find wrong in others. They always do the evil things they want to do. They boast about themselves. The only reason they say good things about others is to get what they want (Jude 1:16 ERV).

Discontent is a manifestation of pride. It flows from a heart that says, *"I deserve better than God has given me."* This was the original sin of Satan himself.

In our letter of Jude, we have a reference to angels who, like Satan, were not content to be the servants of God, "Angels who did not stay within their own position of authority but left their proper dwelling" (Jude 1:6 ERV).

Pride led some angels to say, "We deserve better than God has given to us!" God gave them positions of authority, but they were not content. They are not content now. They never will be. I deserve better than God has given me! *If I catch myself thinking like that, I have to take myself in hand. I have to say to myself,* that is the opposite of everything I believe! I have to remind myself of the Word of God. God has loved me. God gave his Son for me. (John 3:16–18) God has blessed me with every spiritual blessing in Christ (Ephesians 1:3–5). He has given me all that I need for life and godliness (2 Peter 1:3 ERV).

2. Discontent is an expression of rebellion.

In the Old Testament, we have the story of Job, a good and godly man who was greatly blessed by God. His family was blessed, and his business was blessed. Job was living the dream, and then one day, through a series of disasters, he lost everything. Job said, "The Lord gave, and the Lord has taken away; blessed be the name of the Lord" (Job 1:21 ERV).

The discontented person says something different. The discontented person says, "The Lord gave, but he should have given more," or "The Lord has taken away, and he should not have done that." Jude talks about "harsh things that ungodly sinners have spoken against God" (Jude 1:16 ERV).

Discontent is a sin because, at its heart, it is an expression of rebellion against God. The clay says to the potter, "Why have you made me like this?" (Romans 9:20). "God, you should have done something different!" That's rebellion, and the Scripture says, "Who are you to speak like that to God?" (Romans 9:20 ERV).

3. Discontent is a fruit of unbelief.

You see this in Exodus 17. God's people had been greatly blessed. He brought them out of slavery in Egypt, and he provided manna to feed them in the wilderness. Often, those who are most blessed are most discontented!

Then God's people came to a place where there was no water. Now that is a legitimate concern. And there are times in life when we may have legitimate concerns about how God will supply what we need. But their legitimate concern turned into unbelief. They tested the Lord by saying, "Is the Lord among us or not?" (Genesis 17:7 ERV).

They were redeemed people, but they lost confidence that God was with them. If you no longer believe that God is with you, you will no longer be confident that he will supply what you need. And it will not be long before the grumbling begins, and you find yourself sliding into the sin of discontent.

Deal with discontent. I hope you are in a place of saying, "I didn't think too much about this before, but now I see that I need to deal with this sin wherever it rears its ugly head in my life. I need to get beyond the idea that moaning and complaining don't matter. I need to get serious about moving from anger to peace, from frustration to satisfaction, and from anxiety to trust."

Thank God there is a Savior (1 John 4:14 KJV): "And we have seen and do testify that the Father sent the Son to be the *Saviour of the world.*" And in John 4:42 KJV, we read:" And said unto the woman, now we believe, not because of thy saying: for we have heard him ourselves, and know that this is indeed the Christ, the *Saviour of the world.*") to whom we can come. Ask him to forgive this sin if you see it in your life today. Ask him to cleanse you and wash this from your heart. Then ask him to help you grow in contentment.

If you do, then you will find the following:

- Peace in life comes from knowing that everything that concerns you is in the hands of the Savior who loves you (John 14:27).

- Satisfaction lies in knowing that in Jesus Christ, you have all you need (Philippians 4:13).
- Trust begins when you know that he is faithful and those who look to him are never put to shame (1 John 1:9).

It is possible to overcome sin, but we cannot do it on our own. We need God's help. "But there is a great difference between Adam's sin and God's gracious gift. For the sin of this one man, Adam's DNA, brought death to many. But even greater is God's wonderful grace and his gift of forgiveness to many through this other man, Jesus Christ" (Romans 5:15 New Living Translation).

So how do we protect ourselves? The Bible clearly teaches that you must be born again (John 3:3, 6, 7, 16).

> Jesus answered and said unto him, "Verily, verily, I say unto thee, Except a man be born again, he cannot see the kingdom of God. That which is born of the flesh is flesh; and that which is born of the Spirit is spirit. Marvel not that I said unto thee, Ye must be born again. For God so loved the world, that he gave his only begotten Son, that whosoever believeth in him should not perish, but have everlasting life."

Lastly, we read in 2 Corinthian 5:17:

> Therefore if any man be in Christ, he is a new creature: old things are passed away; behold, all things are become new. New Life is for everyone who believes.

How can I know if something is a sin?

Thankfully, we have two facts in our lives to help define and know what sin is. The first fact is *the Word of God, the Bible*, and the second is *the Spirit of God, the Holy Spirit.*

God's word is clear in defining things that are black and white and the bad things that are sinful without any question or room for debate.

We read in Galatians 5:19–21:

> The things your sinful old self wants to do are: committing sexual sin, being morally bad, wild living, doing all kinds of shameful things worshiping false gods, witchcraft, hating, fighting, being jealous, being angry, arguing, dividing into little groups and thinking the other groups are wrong, false teaching, wanting something someone else has, killing other people, using strong drink, wild parties, and all things like these. I told you before and I am telling you again that those who do these things will not have a part in God's kingdom.

The Bible Teaches Us In

- "Who can understand his errors? cleanse thou me from secret faults" (Psalm 19:12)
- "Jesus called the people to Him again. He said, "Listen to Me, all of you, and understand this. It is not what goes into a man's mouth from the outside that makes his mind and heart sinful. It is what comes out from the inside that makes him sinful. You have ears, then listen!" (Mark 7:14–15, 21–23).

> And Jesus said, "The things that make people wrong are the things that come from the inside. All these bad things begin inside a person, in the mind: bad thoughts, sexual sins, stealing, murder, adultery, greed, doing bad things to people, lying, doing things that are morally wrong, jealousy, insulting people, proud talking, and foolish living. These evil things come from inside

a person. And these are the things that make people unacceptable to God."

- For thus saith the LORD, Thy bruise is incurable, and thy wound is grievous. *(You people have a wound that cannot be cured)* There is *none to plead thy cause, that thou mayest be bound up: thou hast no* healing medicines. *(There is none to argue your case, there is no cure for your sickness, so you will not be healed)* For I will restore health unto thee, and I will heal thee of thy wounds, saith the LORD... (Jeremiah 30:12–13, 17).

Please notice the medical language here conveys the idea that sin is terminal. It cannot be cured by being good or being religious or anything else. Beware of putting our confidence in useless cures while our sin spreads and causes us pain. God alone can cure the disease of sin, but we must be willing to let him do it.

Now let's get to the root of our problems:

1. *We have to get to the root.*

    Keep thy heart with all diligence; for out of it are the issues of life. Another words *guard your heart above all else, for it determines the course of your life.* (Proverbs 4:23)

2. *Our heart determines the course of our lives.*

    Sick heart = Sick life
    Healthy heart = Healthy life

3. *Our heart is highly valuable.* We don't guard something that's worth nothing.
    When something is *valuable,* we guard it. We protect it.
    And God says guard it!
    But why would we need to guard our hearts?

4. Our heart is under attack. Just like bacteria can attack our physical bodies, there is a real assault on your heart and my heart. The very nature of the words "guard your heart" indicates that there is something we have to guard *against.* The Bible is clear that we have enemies.

The enemy, the world and our minds, will try to deceive us into thinking

- that we deserve to walk in unforgiveness
- that no one understands our pain
- we deserve to have negative emotions
- we are entitled to worry
- exhibit unforgiveness
- show outrageous anger!

Stay alert! Watch out for your great enemy, the devil.

> Be sober, be vigilant; because your adversary the devil, as a roaring lion, walketh about, seeking whom he may devour. (1 Peter 5:8)

> For we wrestle not against flesh and blood, but against principalities, against powers, against the rulers of the darkness of this world, against spiritual wickedness in high *places.* (Ephesians 6:12)

5. *Our heart is sick.* Not only do we face the enemies around us, but God reveals perhaps the greatest battle lies *within* us.

> The heart *is* deceitful above all *things,* and desperately wicked: who can know it?

> I the LORD search the heart, *I* try the reins, even to give every man according to his ways, *and* according to the fruit of his doings.
>
> In other words, who can understand the human heart? There is nothing else so deceitful! I the LORD search the heart, I try the reins, even to give every man according to his ways, and according to the fruit of his doings. I the LORD search the heart and *examine the mind*!

- The heart is deceitful above all things *and beyond cure*. Who can understand it?
- The heart is hopelessly dark and deceitful- "it is too sick to be healed."
- A puzzle that no one can figure out.

  But I, God says, I search the heart and examine the mind.
- I get to the heart of the human.
- I get to the root of things.
- I treat them as they really are, not as they pretend to be.

6. *We have a HEART PROBLEM.*

> And when he had called all the people *unto him*, he said unto them, Hearken unto me every one *of you*, and understand:
>
> There is nothing from without a man, that entering into him can defile him: but the things which come out of him, those are they that defile the man.
>
> And he said, That which cometh out of the man, that defileth the man.
>
> For from within, *out of the heart of men*, proceed evil thoughts, adulteries, fornications, murders,

> Thefts, covetousness, wickedness, deceit, lasciviousness, an evil eye, blasphemy, pride, foolishness:
>
> All these evil things come from within and defile the man. (Mark 7:14–15, 21–23)

I believe if we misunderstand the root of our problem, we will miss TRUE and COMPLETE healing! It is like trying to treat cancer with a Band-Aid. In many well-meaning Christians, *our first line of attack is to address our thoughts. Yet Jesus just told us that our sinful, unhealthy thoughts originate from our sick hearts! Our hearts are ground zero.*

If not careful, we can make the common mistake of tackling the thoughts but missing the heart. We become aware of our messed-up thinking, but we never stop to examine what's *behind* the messed-up thinking!

However, there are some gray areas of Scripture where something might be sinful for one person and not for another. I will give you a personal example. There are certain shows on television that I cannot watch that I know other Christians do watch. It might be alright for them, but for me, the Holy Spirit has steered me away from those things. This is why your relationship with God is so important because he knows what is best for you.

God's word will define the sins that are black and white, and the Holy Spirit will define for you the sins that are gray. Together, they will keep you from missing the mark and continue living a life pleasing to God.

How is Jesus the solution to our sin problem? The Bible explains it as, "For God made Christ, who never sinned, to be the offering for our sin, so that He could make us right with God through Christ" (2 Corinthians 5:21).

Jesus's sacrifice "cleanses us from all sin" (1 John 1:7), which means "we are no longer slaves to sin" (Romans 6:6) and makes it possible for us to enter heaven.

Ephesians 1:7 says, "In Him we have redemption through His blood, the forgiveness of sins, in accordance with the riches of God's grace." Jesus paid our debt for us so we could be forgiven.

All you have to do is ask God to forgive you through Jesus, believing that Jesus died to pay for your forgiveness–and He will forgive you.

John 3:16–17 contains this wonderful message, "For God so loved the world that He gave His one and only Son, that whoever believes in Him shall not perish but have eternal life. For God did not send His Son into the world to condemn the world, but to save the world through Him."

The healthiest people realize how sick they are, and they run to the Savior.

He is our rock, healer, deliverer, and our salvation.

Understanding True Freedom in Faith!

Understanding freedom according to the Bible is crucial because it offers a deeper perspective on what true freedom means. The Bible talks about freedom in a unique way:

1. *Freedom from sin.* The Bible teaches that true freedom isn't just doing whatever you want but being free from the slavery of sin. It's about being released from the power and guilt of wrongdoing.

   Believers are encouraged to live in righteousness and holiness, which leads to freedom from the guilt and power of sin. In John 8:36, Jesus states, "So if the Son sets you free, you will be free indeed."
2. *Freedom through Christ.* Biblical freedom highlights liberation through Christ. It's about finding freedom by following God's teachings and living in alignment with His will. It's not about being controlled by desires or selfishness but being guided by love and righteousness.

   Galatians 5:1 states, "It is for freedom that Christ has set us free. Stand firm, then, and do not let yourselves be burdened again by a yoke of slavery." This freedom is the result of God's grace and forgiveness.
3. *Freedom to love and serve.* Ironically, the Bible speaks of freedom in the context of servitude. It's about being liber-

ated to serve others selflessly, reflecting Christ's love in our actions.

The Bible emphasizes that freedom in Christ is not about pursuing self-indulgence but about serving others in love. Galatians 5:13 states, "You, my brothers and sisters, were called to be free. But do not use your freedom to indulge the flesh; rather, serve one another humbly in love."

4. *Freedom in responsibility.* Understanding biblical freedom means accepting responsibility. It's about making choices that honor God and contribute positively to society, recognizing that true freedom doesn't mean escaping consequences.
5. *Freedom from fear.* It's about being released from fear—fear of judgment, fear of the future, fear of inadequacy. Biblical freedom offers a sense of peace and security that comes from a relationship with God.
6. *Freedom in truth.* The Bible encourages freedom in truth, emphasizing that knowing and embracing truth brings liberation. It's not about believing whatever you wish but finding real freedom in God's eternal truths.
7. *Freedom in Christ's redemption.* Ultimately, biblical freedom stems from the redemption provided by Christ's sacrifice. It's about being set free from the bondage of sin and death, offering a new life in Him.
8. *Freedom of conscience.* The Bible acknowledges the importance of freedom of conscience, Romans 14 discusses how believers should respect one another's consciences in matters that are not explicitly commanded by God. Honoring the Lord in all we do.
9. *Political freedom.* While the primary focus of the Bible is spiritual freedom, there are instances where it acknowledges the importance of political freedom. For example, the Bible encourages respect for governing authorities (Romans 13) while also promoting justice and righteousness.

10. *Freedom from the law.* The New Testament teaches that believers are no longer under the law but under grace (Romans 6:14).

    Understanding biblical freedom helps us comprehend the depth of spiritual liberty, offering a perspective that transcends mere earthly freedoms. It guides us to live in harmony with God's purpose, leading to a truly fulfilled and liberated life.

What Is Freedom?

We are living in a world filled with all sorts of evil, including crime, war, terrorism, racism, and all manner of societal woes. The snowball effect occurs as evil happens and provokes yet another act of evil and hatred. As things intensify, many are asking why evil is in the world.

Freedom, as understood in the Bible, has several layers of meaning. Here are some key aspects of freedom according to the Bible:

True freedom is found in Christ—freedom from sin and the opportunity to live in righteousness and love.

Furthermore, the Bible records that evil exists in the world because of two primary sources. The devil (referred to as Satan hereafter) is a primary source and has free reign to unleash evil in the world. Secondly, the human heart tends toward sin and wickedness. Many blame God for the bad things that happen, but He is the cure, not the cause of evil.

> Satan started in heaven but wanted more power. His pride got him kicked out, and now he causes trouble on earth. He tempted Adam and Eve, bringing sin into our hearts for the first time. We all have that struggle inside us, even if we think we're good. The Bible says our hearts are tricky and sick. Admitting our mistakes is important. If we do, God forgives us and makes us clean.

The Human Heart Contains Evil

The story of Adam and Eve is one most of us know. Satan disguised himself as a snake and convinced Eve to eat the forbidden fruit. The action of eating the forbidden fruit allowed sin to enter the human heart for the first time.

We now have to contend with our hearts as well as the hearts of others and the evil that comes from it. You may think you are a good person, certainly compared to fill in the blank. Yet the Bible is clear that all of us are plagued with the same issue. Jeremiah 17:9 (ESV) says, "The heart is deceitful above all things, and desperately sick, who can understand it?" Other translations say "desperately wicked" rather than "desperately sick."

The Bible declares in 1 John 1:8–10 KJV:

> If we say that we have no sin, we deceive ourselves, and the truth is not in us.
>
> If we confess our sins, he is faithful and just to forgive us our sins, and to cleanse us from all unrighteousness. If we say that we have not sinned, we make him a liar, and his word is not in us.

Why Doesn't God Stop the Evil in the World?

Simply put, God has given us free will to make the right choices.

We are all born as sinners and fall short of the glory of God (Romans 3:23). That inclines us to sin (to do and think wrong things). It is the power of Christ in us that allows us to turn from sin to resist the influence of Satan and our thoughts and desires.

Not only can you resist your temptations to do evil, but you can become an influencer of good, not evil. Just as evil speech and actions beget more of the same, it is likewise true positive speech and actions snowball in society and begin to hold back the tide of evil. The "power of Christ" that we need comes from the indwelling of the Holy Spirit, given to us when we accept Christ as our Savior.

Remember, we live in a fallen world with all the ills that it naturally entails. The fall of man has brought not just separation from the truth, life, freedom, right, liberty, and God but also sicknesses of various types. Many of these illnesses are emotional and mental rather than physical.

Satan's fall and influence.

- Satan, once a high-ranking figure in heaven, desired worship like God and rebelled.
- He was cast out but still holds power on Earth, influencing humans since the time of Adam and Eve.
- Despite his limited time, he continues to affect those who don't seek God's protection.

The human heart and sin.

- The story of Adam and Eve illustrates how sin entered humanity.
- Everyone struggles with sin; our hearts are prone to deceit and wickedness.

Free will and God's role.

- God grants free will; we're born sinners but empowered by Christ to resist evil.
- Positive actions combat evil, and Christ's power within us helps us resist temptation.

The inner conflict.

- The battle within ourselves between doing good and evil is a constant struggle.
- Sin enslaves us, but living by the Spirit guides us toward righteousness.

Guarding the heart.

- The heart signifies the mind and will, where decisions originate.
- Guarding it means filtering thoughts and focusing on positive, truthful, and noble things.

Seeking God's help and truth.

- In hard times, turning to God brings comfort and strength.
- The Spirit of Truth guides us; Jesus represents truth and freedom.

Temptations and overcoming evil.

- Satan tempts through desires of the flesh, eyes, and pride of life.
- Overcoming temptation involves understanding the truth and seeking God's guidance.

Choosing freedom in truth.

- Embracing truth, learning from Scripture, and praying help combat confusion and bring freedom from sin.
- Surrendering to God's way leads to experiencing His salvation and blessings.

Prayer for guidance and change.

- Personal prayers asking for understanding, transformation, and guidance help align with God's will.
- Following His ways leads to a transformed life and a deeper relationship with Him.

Assurance in God's protection.

- No matter what, God cares for us and supports us through challenges.
- Confidence in God's love and presence offers strength and security in every situation.

The War Inside Us
Freedom Starts There!

We read in Romans 7:15–20:

> I don't understand why I act the way I do. I don't do the good I want to do, and I do the evil I hate. And if I don't want to do what I do, that means I am not free But I am not really the one doing the evil. It is sin living in me that does it. So if I do what I don't want to do, then I am not really the one doing it. It is the sin living in me that does it.

> Jesus answered them, "Truly, truly, I say to you, everyone who commits sin is a slave to sin." (John 8:34)

In other words, Jesus said, "The truth is, everyone who sins is a slave—a slave to sin." Not free!

> For those who live according to the flesh have their outlook shaped by the things of the flesh, but those who live according to the Spirit have their outlook shaped by the things of the Spirit. (Romans 8:5)

I have learned in my life that the enemy, the evil around us, and our negative self-talk like to attack us daily by telling us lies contrary to God's Word.

Thoughts of worry, doubt, and fear have the power to consume our minds, causing us to lose hope. When you begin to have these feelings, it's hard to detect God's truth from the enemy's lies. You need to remind yourself of the Word of God and choose the Word of God over that doubt, fear, worry, or view!

Our minds are a battlefield where good thoughts and bad thoughts are constantly fighting for our attention. *Proverbs 4:23 says, "Keep thy heart with all diligence, for out of it are issues of life."* It is up to you and me to filter what thoughts you choose to entertain.

For that reason, the Bible tells us to "think on good things" (Philippians 4:8). If you allow the cares of life to consume you, sadness and depression are soon to follow. Anxiety in your heart has the power to weigh you down. (Proverbs 12:25).

It is comforting to know that God, through His Holy Spirit, empowers you to fight a good fight and have victory. Furthermore, it is very comforting to discover and realize that you can have a victory in any battle. The scripture tells us we can share all our cares and worries with God because He cares for us (1 Peter 5:7).

Why does the Bible say "Guard your hearts"?

In the human body, the heart is essential for living. I am not a doctor or scientist, and I've never played one on TV either, but what little I know about human biology is this: when the heart stops, you stop.

The beat of the heart is proof and evidence that you are still alive. Whenever you watch shows where there is an accident or trauma, when the paramedics show up, the first thing they do is check for a pulse. Again, no pulse, no life.

Clearly, this shows how important the heart is to human living. Yet, as Christians, you don't just have a human heart that produces physical life. You also have a spiritual heart that produces spiritual life. It is this heart that leads us to this verse in Proverbs 4:23. Right off the bat, this verse lifts the importance of the heart by instructing us to guard it.

What I want to help you understand is why you should guard your heart as Proverbs 4:23 instructs you to do? I believe as you begin to understand the verse, the why will become clearer.

To begin with, let's see what is meant by the heart. When the Bible speaks about the heart, it is not talking about the physical heart that beats. It refers to the mind, the will, or even the inner man. The mind and the will are the places where we make our life decisions. Every choice we make and everything we decide to do comes from a decision of our will or our mind.

That's why salvation has to be a decision of your mind. "If you declare with your mouth, 'Jesus is Lord,' and believe in your heart that God raised him from the dead, you will be saved. For it is with your heart that you believe and are justified, and it is with your mouth that you profess your faith and are saved" (Romans 10:9–10).

Surprisingly enough, that word in the New Testament means mind, will, or inner man. So as we can see, the heart plays an important role in our decision making, starting with the decision to follow Jesus.

Because of this, we now see the importance of this verse. Since everything we do flows out of our mind, then it makes sense to put a hedge or guard around it so we can protect the things we do.

There is an old computer saying, I don't even know if they use this anymore, but it was GIGO. This stands for garbage in, garbage out. If you put garbage programming into a computer, you are going to get garbage outputs.

The heart works exactly the same way. Our decisions and choices are a result of the things we feed our hearts or our minds. If we put the right stuff in, we will get the right stuff out, but the reverse of this is also true.

Guarding our hearts is making sure we are keeping the wrong influences out because these things will ultimately affect the decisions we make.

Here is a verse that sums up how to guard our hearts.

> Finally, brothers and sisters, whatever is true, whatever is noble, whatever is right, whatever is pure, whatever is lovely, whatever is admirable—if anything is excellent or praiseworthy—think about such things. (Philippians 4:8)

Remember, the heart refers to our mind and our will. If we follow the prescription of Philippians and think about these types of things, it will influence our actions. We will not only guard our hearts, but we will see a difference in everything we do.

Dear family and friends, during hard times, it is a natural response to turn to family and friends for support and encouragement. And we should. Although having these relationships is important, God should always be the first person we turn to.

We must learn this truth in our lives. No matter what type of help you need, your Heavenly Father has all the power, and there is nothing too hard for Him (Jeremiah 32:17).

When it comes to fighting for you, other humans will fall short against the Almighty power of God. If you rely on Him, you will always win. Even when you don't see Him, you can be comforted knowing that God always has your best interest at heart.

He has your back! When you feel alone, He is there waiting for you to call on Him. Through prayer, tell God how you feel and ask Him for what you need (Philippians 4:6–7). Your Heavenly Father loves you, and He is always ready to answer when you call Him. We read this in Jeremiah 33:3 KJV.

> Call unto me, and I will answer thee, and show thee great and mighty things, which thou knowest not.

God has your back, and He wants you to believe He will keep His Word concerning you.

In Isaiah 40:10, it reads, "So do not fear, for I am with you; do not be dismayed, for I am your God. I will strengthen you and help you; I will uphold you with my righteous right hand." It means, "I've got your back."

> To understand freedom, we need to understand the Spirit of Error and the Spirit of the Truth regarding freedom. (1 John 4:6)

But first, let us discover the spirit of error.

Remember, the Bible records that evil exists in the world because of two primary sources. *The devil* (referred to as Satan hereafter) is a primary source and has free reign to unleash evil in the world. Second, the human heart tends toward sin and wickedness. Many blame God for the bad things that happen, but He is the cure, not the cause of evil.

The devil's master plan is to use the human heart, which tends toward sin and wickedness against us, to promote evil.

The devil tempts us in three ways!

Yes, Satan has many strategies, schemes, and devices to deceive us.

But the devil always tempts us in three following ways: *lust of the flesh, lust of the eyes, and pride of life.* He may tempt us with sins of the flesh, such as immorality, pleasure-seeking, and destructive habits. If those don't work, he may tempt us with sins of the heart or mind, such as evil thoughts, wrong motives, anger, and jealousy.

Sinful lust is an overpowering desire for that which God has forbidden.

We read in 1 John 2:15–16 KJV:

> Do not love the world or anything in the world. If anyone loves the world, love for the Father is not in them. For everything in the world—the lust of the flesh, the lust of the eyes, and the pride of life—comes not from the Father but from the world.

The lust of the eyes occurs when we see something visually that provokes covetousness, jealousy, or sexual lust.

The pride of life is the desire in every human being to be his or her own god. Arrogance, self-promotion, and greed all stem from the pride of life.

The lust of the flesh is also one foe we fight, such as immorality, pleasure-seeking, and destructive habits.

Satan and his demons are constantly tempting human beings to sin against God, and the Bible gives us many examples. The devil "walketh around like a roaring lion seeking whom he may devour" (1 Peter 5:8). Satan fills people's hearts with lies (Acts 5:3). He is "the tempter" (1 Thessalonians 3:5). In Satan's temptation of Eve in Genesis 3 and in his temptation of Jesus in Matthew 4, we see the tactics he used and still uses with us. While varied in their details, most temptations fall into one of three categories listed in 1 John 2:16: the lust of the flesh, the lust of the eyes, and the pride of life. In Satan's first temptation of Jesus, he appealed to the lust of the flesh. Jesus was very hungry, and Satan tempted Him to use His power to make bread for Himself. Jesus resisted the temptation, but the encounter shows that Satan does not play fair. He exploits our physical weaknesses and kicks us when we're down. He knows the weak places in our flesh and looks for opportunities to stir illicit passions inside our hearts. When Satan tempted Eve to eat the forbidden fruit, he suggested to her that the Lord was keeping something delicious from her (Genesis 3:6). When he tempts us with the lust of the flesh, he points to a natural desire and suggests that we should meet it in our own selfish way. Eve's natural desire for food was not wrong, but Satan exploited it. That desire became sin when she fulfilled it in an ungodly way. Sexual immorality begins with a natural desire for intimacy. But if we have not allowed Jesus to become a greater passion, the tempter may convince us that we must meet this need our own way. The second way Satan tempts us is through the lust of the eyes. Eve's eyes told her something about the fruit that conflicted with what God had said about it. Eve's eyes rebelled against God's commandment and "saw that the fruit of the tree was good for food and pleasing to the eye" (Genesis 3:6).

Our eyes play a major role in our decision-making. We see something we want, and our flesh agrees that we must have it. In this age of visual overstimulation, our eyes take in millions of bits of information throughout the day, and unless we filter that information through a pure heart (Matthew 5:8; Psalm 24:4), our eyes will lead us into sin. Samson started his downhill slide with the lust of the eyes. Judges 14–16 details Samson's flirtation with sin and the tragic results. As God's chosen leader, Samson had no business hanging out in Philistine territory, much less flirting with their women. But his eyes led him into sin: "Then Samson went down to Timnah and saw...one of the daughters of the Philistines. So he came back and told his father and mother, 'I saw a woman... Get her for me, for *she looks good to me*" (Judges 14:1–3; emphasis added, NASB).

When Satan tempted Jesus, he tried to get the Son of God to lust with His eyes, showing the Lord all the kingdoms of the world and offering to give Him everything—without the cross. Jesus defeated Satan's temptation with the Word of God (Luke 4:8; Deuteronomy 6:13). Despite what His eyes saw, Jesus would not be swayed by it. Therefore, in Jesus's case, Satan could not exploit the lust of the eyes. The pride of life is a weakness we all yield to at times. Satan tempts us with the desire to be our own gods, and he is skillful at rubbing our egos. Eve's desire to be made wise led her to sin in Genesis 3. In her pride of life, she rejected the Lord's right to rule over her and chose instead to make her own decisions. In essence, she became her own god.

Christians can play into Satan's hands when we hold out on full surrender to the lordship of Jesus. We tend to give more consideration to pleasing other people than to pleasing God. We like to retain "veto power," just in case God wants us to do something we don't want to do. Satan tempted Jesus with the pride of life in Luke 4:9–11. He gave Jesus an opportunity to "show off" and publicly prove that He was the Son of God. The act would involve a spectacular miracle, the Father's care, and many angels. Jesus's response to Satan's third temptation was to again quote Scripture (Luke 4:12; cf. Deuteronomy 6:16). Satan tempts us in many ways, but "we are not unaware of his schemes" (2 Corinthians 2:11). We know he pretenses as an angel of light (2 Corinthians 11:14), trying to make evil look good. We know he manipulates with false guilt, exploits natural weaknesses, and twists Scripture. We know he deceives, distracts, and destroys. He has many fiery darts, but they are all quenched with the shield of faith (Ephesians 6:16). We can overcome the temptations of Satan because "the one who is in you is greater than the one who is in the world" (1 John 4:4). Satan may tempt us through the lust of the flesh, but we "do not walk according to the flesh, but according to the Spirit" (Romans 8:4). Satan may tempt us through the lust of the eyes, but our prayer is "Turn my eyes away from worthless things; preserve my life according to your word" (Psalm 119:37). Satan may tempt us through the pride of life, but we humble ourselves continually before the Lord (1 Peter 5:6; James 4:10).

Please note the following list is all the desires that come from the spirit of error within us, the unresolved desires that *promote fun and freedom but turns us into slaves of corruption.*

For whatever overcomes a person, to that he is enslaved, the exact opposite of freedom (2 Peter 2:19)!

- The lust of the flesh—love of self (2 Timothy 3:2)
- Lust of the eyes—love of the pleasure (2 Timothy 3:4)
- Pride of life—love of the money (1 Timothy 6:10)
- Love of power
- Love of fame
- Love of recognition
- Love of sexuality
- Love of covetousness
- Love of adultery, fornication, uncleanness, lasciviousness, idolatry, witchcraft, hatred, variance, emulations, wrath, strife, seditions, heresies, envying, murders, drunkenness, and reveling!

Now let us discover the spirit of truth and life. The fact is that the spirit of truth never tempts us or deceives us because it is written that the Spirit-Word of the Lord is pure and righteous altogether— and stands fast forever and ever. We read in Psalm 19:7–9 (Easy-to-Read Version):

> The LORD's teachings are perfect. They give strength to his people. The LORD's rules can be trusted. They help even the foolish become wise. The LORD's laws are right. They make people happy.

The LORD's commands are good. They show people the right way to live.

Learning respect for the LORD is good. It will last forever. The LORD's judgments are right. They are completely fair.

Jesus said to him, "*I am the way, and the truth, and the life*. No one comes to the Father except through me." (John 14:6)

And you will know the truth, and the truth will set you free. (John 8:32)

When the Spirit of truth comes, he will guide you into all the truth, for he will not speak on his own authority, but whatever he hears he will speak, and he will declare to you the things that are to come. (John 16:13)

Sanctify them in the truth; *your word is truth*. (John 17:17)

God is spirit, and those who worship him must worship in spirit and *truth*. (John 4:24)

Do your best to present yourself to God as one approved, a worker who has no need to be ashamed, rightly handling *the word of truth*. (2 Timothy 2:15)

Stand therefore, having fastened on *the belt of truth*, and having put on the breastplate of righteousness. (Ephesians 6:14)

Little children, let us not love in word or talk but in deed and *in truth*. (1 John 3:18)

The Lord is near to all who call on him, to all who call on him in *truth.* (Psalm 145:18)

The sum of your word is *truth*, and every one of your righteous rules endures forever. (Psalm 119:160)

Lead me in your truth and teach me, for you are the God of my salvation; for you I wait all the day long. (Psalm 25:5)

And the Word became flesh and dwelt among us, and we have seen his glory, glory as of the only Son from the Father, full of grace and *truth*. (John 1:14)

Love is patient and kind; love does not envy or boast; it is not arrogant or rude. It does not insist on its own way; it is not irritable or resentful; it does not rejoice at wrongdoing, but rejoices with *the truth*. (1 Corinthians 13:4–6)

Of his own will he brought us forth by *the word of truth*, that we should be a kind of first fruits of his creatures. (James 1:18)

Rather, *speaking the truth* in love, we are to grow up in every way into him who is the head, into Christ. (Ephesians 4:15)

For the law was given through Moses; grace and *truth* came through Jesus Christ. (John 1:17)

Then Pilate said to him, "So you are a king?" Jesus answered, "You say that I am a king. For this purpose I was born and for this purpose I have come into the world—to bear witness to

> the *truth*. Everyone who is of the truth listens to my voice." Pilate said to him, "What is truth?" After he had said this, he went back outside to the Jews and told them, "I find no guilt in him." (John 18:37–38)

> Teach me your way, O Lord, that I may *walk in your truth*; unite my heart to fear your name. (Psalm 86:11)

> And we know that the Son of God has come and has given us understanding, so that we may know him *who is true*; and we are in him who is true, in his Son Jesus Christ. *He is the true God and eternal life.* (1 John 5:20)

> For you were called to freedom. Only do not use your freedom as an opportunity for the flesh, but through love serve one another. (Galatians 5:15)

> Now the works of the flesh are manifest, which are these, Adultery, fornication, uncleanness, lasciviousness, idolatry, witchcraft, hatred, variance, emulations, wrath, strife, seditions, heresies,
>
> Envying, murders, drunkenness, raveling's, and such like: of the which I tell you before, as I have also told you in time past, that they which do such things shall not inherit the kingdom of God. (Galatians 5:19–21)

God wants us to be FREE from sin (Romans 6:18; *being then made free from sin).*

God wants us to be changed in our thoughts, views, attitudes, and in our actions and deeds by the Holy *Spirit. God always offers us a way of escape, even when we get ourselves into deep trouble by going our own ways, by believing in a lie, even when we think there is no way out!*

The farther we drift from God, the more confused our thinking becomes! When we forget to include Him in our daily lives, we will lose our purpose, and soon, we will do what is right in our own eyes, and we will be shocked at what we are capable of doing (Judges 19:1–30).

Let us not mistakenly *depart from God's Will and from the Word of God.* Let us not put the Lord to the side in our lives! Let us bring Him into every part of our lives for our own sanity.

God's solution and steps to our healthy recovery are always the same:

- *Admitting we have rebelled against God—it changes our thoughts!*
- *Forsaking our sinful direction—it changes our attitude!*
- *Seeking to live as God instructs us in His Word—it changes our actions!*

The following are my personal discoveries regarding my responsibilities for letting the Holy Spirit of God bring biblical changes to my life!

Every day, the enemy and negative thoughts bombard us with lies, causing worry and fear. These feelings cloud our minds, making it hard to distinguish between God's truth and the enemy's lies. To fight this, remind yourself of God's Word and choose it over doubt and fear.

Our minds are a battleground where good and bad thoughts clash. Proverbs 4:23 emphasizes guarding our hearts because our thoughts shape our lives. The Bible urges us to focus on positive things (Philippians 4:8), as dwelling on worries leads to sadness and depression (Proverbs 12:25).

God, through His Spirit, empowers us to win battles and overcome. We can share all our worries with Him because He cares (1 Peter 5:7).

Why guard your heart? The heart in the Bible refers to our mind and will—the seat of our decisions. Since our actions flow from our minds, it's vital to protect our thoughts. What we fill our minds with shapes our choices.

Garbage in, garbage out—the heart works similarly. Guarding it means filtering negative influences that can impact our decisions.

Philippians 4:8 outlines how to guard our hearts—focus on what's true, noble, right, pure, lovely, admirable, excellent, or praiseworthy. This will influence our actions positively.

During tough times, turning to family and friends is natural, but God should be our first choice. He has all the power and cares deeply for us (Jeremiah 32:17). Rely on Him; He always has your best interest at heart.

God promises to answer when we call on Him (Jeremiah 33:3) and assures us of His constant presence and support (Isaiah 40:10).

Understanding freedom means recognizing the spirit of error and the spirit of truth (1 John 4:6).

Remember, dear family and friends, when we get saved, we are born again with the life of God. But this new life is only the beginning of our spiritual journey. After we are born again, the next step is to consecrate or give ourselves to the Lord, which means surrendering ourselves to the Lord.

Why should we consecrate and give ourselves to the Lord? To walk in the Lord's way.

Before we were saved, we took our own way, made our own decisions, and chose the direction for our lives. After we're saved, God wants us to walk in His way and be led by Him.

But if we don't give ourselves to Him, how can we know what His way is? How can He lead us? Consecrating, giving ourselves to Him keeps us in His way and saves us from taking our own way.

We can pray, "Lord, I don't want to make my own decisions alone anymore. I want to team up with you. I want to be kept in Your way. So, Lord Jesus, I give myself to You."

Surrendering ourselves to the Lord is the door for us to enter through to enjoy all the riches of God's salvation. When we give ourselves to the Lord, He will lead us in our experience into the enjoyment of the rich blessings of God's full salvation.

"Lord, here I am. I give myself to You fully. I belong to You. Lead me by Your Spirit into the experience and enjoyment of all You have for me in Your salvation." When we do this, we will be kept in

God's way, grow in His life, allow Him to work in us, and know that He has our back.

To have confidence that God has my back, in good times and in bad times, I have learned to pray through the Scriptures each day for forty days. This is what it takes to bring changes into our lives and to be united with God.

What better words could we choose to express to our Father than the very Words He has given to us in the Bible?

As you read the Word of God from the Bible, God is speaking to you. When you pray, you are speaking to God.

Do not be afraid. Pray the following prayers with me.

> Lord: I want to examine myself (2 Corinthians 13:5) from your Word (Psalm 139:23–24). Search me, O God, and *know my heart*: try me, and *know my thoughts*: And see if there be any wicked way in me and lead me in the way everlasting.
>
> Search me so that I can see my bad thoughts, my bad desires, my bad feelings, my sick emotions, bad reactions, and my sinful nature so I can confess it to you for healing so that I can get free from those hidden, unhealthy behaviors and attitudes which grieves you and the Holy Spirit, (Ephesians 4:30) so I won't sin against you (Psalm 119:11).
>
> Lord, I want to see deep down why I am not free and I am so powerless and unhappy!
>
> Lord, I want to be changed, healed, and be free from the emotional pain that I am experiencing in my life!
>
> Lord, please open my mind so I can understand the scripture, the Bible! Luke 24:45: "Then

opened he their understanding, that they might understand the scriptures."

Lord, please open my ears so I can hear your voice! Psalm 40:6, "Sacrifice and offering thou didst not desire; *mine ears hast thou opened*: burnt offering and sin offering hast thou not required."

Revelation 2:7: "He that hath an ear, let him hear what the Spirit saith unto the churches; To him that overcometh will I give to eat of the tree of life, which is in the midst of the paradise of God."

Lord, please open my eyes so I can see your miracles!

Psalm 119:18: "Open thou mine eyes, that I may behold wondrous things out of thy law."

Lord, please give me understanding so I can understand the Bible!

Psalm 119:34: "Give me understanding, and I shall keep thy law; yea, I shall observe it with my whole heart."

Lord, please teach me and guide me with your words!

Psalm 119:68: "Thou art good, and doest good; teach me thy statutes."

Lord, I want to live with you every day of my life!

Psalm 101:2–3: "I will behave myself wisely in a perfect way. O when wilt thou come unto me? I will walk within my house with a perfect heart. I will set no wicked thing before mine eyes: I hate the work of them that turn aside; it shall not cleave to me."

Psalm 27:4–5: "One thing have I desired of the Lord, that will I seek after; that I may dwell in the house of the Lord all the days of my life, to behold the beauty of the Lord, and to enquire in his temple. For in the time of trouble he shall hide me in his pavilion: in the secret of his tabernacle shall he hide me; he shall set me up upon a rock."

Proverbs 30:7–9: "Two things have I required of thee; deny me them not before I die: Remove far from me vanity and lies: give me neither poverty nor riches; feed me with food convenient for me: Lest I be full, and deny thee, and say, who is the Lord? Or lest I be poor, and steal, and take the name of my God in vain."

Job 31:1: "I made a covenant with mine eyes; why then should I think upon a maid?"

Psalm 25:15: "Mine eyes are ever toward the Lord; for he shall pluck my feet out of the net."

Psalm 119:112: "I have inclined mine heart to perform thy statutes always, even unto the end."

Psalm 18:28: "For thou wilt light my candle: the Lord my God will enlighten my darkness."

Once the above prayers become part of your life and become the desires of your heart, then I can assure you of many "miracles and changes" will happen in your life!

No matter what happens throughout the season, at school or at home, God has your back. He'll always be there to encourage you, pick you up, and strengthen you. Today, go out into the world with confidence, knowing that the Creator of all things loves you and is watching over you.

Understanding Unveiling God's Plan!

Understanding God's plans according to the Bible involves interpreting various passages and themes found throughout its text. Here are some key aspects of God's plans as represented in the Bible:

1. *Divine sovereignty.* The Bible declares God's sovereignty and control over the universe. He is the Creator and sustainer of all things, and His plans are ultimately in accordance with His will (Isaiah 46:10; Romans 8:28).
2. *Plan of redemption.* A central theme in the Bible is God's plan of redemption through Jesus Christ. According to the Bible, God's plan is to provide salvation and reconciliation for humanity through the death and resurrection of Jesus (John 3:16; Ephesians 1:7).
3. *Covenantal promises.* Throughout the Old Testament, God establishes covenants with various individuals and groups, such as the Abrahamic, Mosaic, and Davidic covenants. These covenants outline God's promises and plans for His people, including blessings and responsibilities (Genesis 12:2–3; Exodus 19:5; 2 Samuel 7:16).
4. *Prophetic messages.* God often communicates His plans through prophets and messengers. The prophetic books in the Bible contain revelations about God's intentions, warnings, and promises (e.g., Isaiah, Jeremiah, and Ezekiel).

5. *Foreknowledge and predestination.* The Bible touches on the concept of God's foreknowledge and predestination, suggesting that God has a plan for individuals and that He knows their destinies in advance (Romans 8:29; Jeremiah 1:5).
6. *God's will and guidance.* The Bible encourages believers to seek God's will and guidance in their lives. Proverbs 3:5–6 advises trusting in the Lord and acknowledging Him in all one's ways to align with His plans.
7. *Human responsibility.* While God has a divine plan; the Bible also emphasizes human responsibility and free will. Individuals are called to make choices in alignment with God's moral and ethical standards (Deuteronomy 30:19; Joshua 24:15).
8. *Mystery and faith.* The Bible acknowledges that God's plans may be mysterious and beyond human comprehension. Faith and trust are essential in understanding and accepting His plans (Isaiah 55:8–9).
9. *End-times prophecy.* The Bible contains prophecies about the end times and God's ultimate plan for the world. This includes the return of Christ, judgment, and the establishment of God's eternal kingdom (Revelation; Daniel 7).

God has a plan for us and everything we do. He created this world with a plan, and He will someday end this world according to His plan. As Christians, it's our job to trust that plan, believe in His will, and lean on Him whenever we feel discouraged or lost. I have decided in my life to trust the Lord, and it's been a wonderful journey for me.

Most importantly, we must always understand God's plan for us is good because it will serve His divine purpose.

In the modern world we live in, we like to question everything and find answers to all our problems. But sometimes, we cannot provide answers, and we should simply trust God's will and have faith.

Understanding God's Plan for You

Many Christians seek to know God's plan for their lives. Questions like "How do I find it?" and "How can I be certain?" arise. However, the Bible offers clear principles about God's will, showing that He wants us to know and follow His plan.

Discovering God's Plan
Bible Principles

The Bible teaches principles applicable to all believers. For instance, Ephesians 6:8 suggests that blessing others leads to receiving blessings from the Lord. Galatians 6:7 explains the law of the harvest: what we sow, we reap.

God's Plan for All Believers

First Thessalonians 5:16–18 emphasizes joy, prayer, and thanksgiving as God's will for every believer, irrespective of circumstances.

Understanding God's Plan
How?

We can know God's plan through His Word. Studying Scripture helps us understand His intentions for our lives (2 Timothy 3:16–17). Romans 12:1–2 encourages us to turn away from worldly patterns and dedicate ourselves to God, allowing our minds to be renewed.

God's Plan Detailed
Holiness and Sanctification

First Thessalonians 4:3–7 outlines God's will for a holy life, including purity and respecting others.

Discovering God's Plan Prayer and Revelation

Colossians 4:12 exemplifies Epaphras praying for believers to discern God's will. Sometimes, God reveals His plans through personal circumstances or dreams, but we must align these revelations with what Scripture says.

Trusting God's Timing and Path

Drawing near to God brings us closer to understanding His plan (James 4:8). Jeremiah 1:5 reassures us that God ordains our paths.

Trusting in God's Universal Plan

God's plan encompasses everything in our lives, as stated in Jeremiah 1:5. Each person has a purpose in God's design, no matter the scale.

Trusting Through Struggles

During hardships, trust and praise God as seen in Habakkuk 3:17–19 KJV.

> Although the fig tree shall not blossom, neither shall fruit be in the vines; the labour of the olive shall fail, and the fields shall yield no meat; the flock shall be cut off from the fold, and there shall be no herd in the stalls: Yet I will rejoice in the LORD, I will joy in the God of my salvation. The LORD God is my strength, and he will make my feet like hinds' feet, and he will make me to walk upon mine high places. To the chief singer on my stringed instruments.

Even in tough times, trust that God's plan won't overwhelm us beyond what we can handle.

Understanding God's Purpose

Many wonder why a loving, all-powerful God allows so much suffering and wrongdoing in the world. Some suggest that God set the universe in motion and left us to run things ourselves. But others, like physicist Conyers Herring, believe in an ongoing force guiding improvements in the world.

God's Plan for Earth and Humanity

Originally, God wanted Earth inhabited by righteous, perfect humans. Isaiah 45:18 says Earth wasn't made for nothing but to be lived in. However, when Adam and Eve rebelled, God adjusted His plan but still wanted humans to fulfill His purpose.

Human Independence and God's Knowledge

God allowed humans for about six thousand years to govern themselves. This revealed our inability to direct our lives without God's guidance, as stated in Jeremiah 10:23 and Ecclesiastes 8:9. God foresaw these outcomes and knew humans couldn't successfully rule over each other.

God's Purpose through the Ages

In God's view, six thousand years are like six days. Second Peter 3:8 explains that God's timing differs from ours. He's patient, desiring everyone to repent (2 Peter 3:9). God allowed time for mankind to fail in governing the world, proving that divine guidance is essential for success (Genesis 2:15–17).

God's Original Plan

God intended earth to be inhabited by perfect humans. Though Adam and Eve's rebellion caused adjustments, it didn't halt His purpose.

Human Independence and God's Foreknowledge

God allowed humans free will, foreseeing their inability to govern themselves (Jeremiah 10:23). The outcomes of man's dominion proved detrimental (Ecclesiastes 8:9).

God's Patience and Plan

Despite appearing as a spectator, God had a reason for not intervening directly. He views thousands of years as brief moments (2 Peter 3:8–9), allowing humans time to realize their limitations.

The Conclusion of Human Rule

The era of human independence is nearing its end. The prophecy foretells the final days of this ungodly system (2 Timothy 3:1–5; Daniel 2:44).

The Coming Kingdom

Armageddon will signal the end of mismanagement without destroying the earth (Revelation 16:14, 16; 11:18). After this, a thousand-year reign under Christ's rule will bring a time of restoration and resurrection (Revelation 20:1–3; Acts 24:15).

God's Glorious Purpose

Ultimately, God's purpose is a world without suffering or death, where tears and pain cease to exist (Revelation 21:4, 5). This fulfillment is imminent (Isaiah 14:24, 27).

Bible Verses About God's Plan

For I know the plans I have for you, declares the LORD, plans to prosper you and not to harm you, plans to give you hope and a future. (Jeremiah 29:11)

Perhaps you were born for such a time as this. (Esther 4:14)

And we know that for those who love God all things work together for good, for those who are called according to his purpose. (Romans 8:28)

The plans of the LORD stand firm forever, the purposes of His heart through all generations. (Psalm 33:11)

The Lord is not slow in keeping his promise, as some understand slowness. Instead, he is patient with you, not wanting anyone to perish, but everyone to come to repentance. (2 Peter 3:9)

I will instruct you and teach you in the way you should go; I will counsel you with my eye upon you. (Psalm 32:8)

Trust in the LORD with all your heart and lean not on your own understanding; in all your ways submit to him, and he will make your paths straight. (Proverbs 3:5–6)

I beseech you therefore, brethren, by the mercies of God, that ye present your bodies a living sacrifice, holy, acceptable unto God, which is your reasonable service. [2] And be not conformed to this world: but be ye transformed by the renewing of your mind, that ye may prove what is that good, and acceptable, and perfect, will of God. (Romans 12:1–2)

For I know the thoughts that I think toward you, saith the LORD, thoughts of peace, and not of evil, to give you an expected end. (Jeremiah 29:11)

But my God shall supply all your need according to his riches in glory by Christ Jesus. (Philippians 4:19)

And God is able to make all grace abound toward you; that ye, always having all sufficiency in all things, may abound to every good work. (2 Corinthians 9:8)

For thou shalt eat the labour of thine hands: happy shalt thou be, and it shall be well with thee. (Psalm 128:2)

This book of the law shall not depart out of thy mouth; but thou shalt meditate therein day and night, that thou mayest observe to do according to all that is written therein: for then thou shalt make thy way prosperous, and then thou shalt have good success. (Joshua 1:8)

And he shall be like a tree planted by the rivers of water, that bringeth forth his fruit in his season; his leaf also shall not wither; and whatsoever he doeth shall prosper. (Psalm 1:3)

Give, and it shall be given unto you; good measure, pressed down, and shaken together, and running over, shall men give into your bosom. For with the same measure that ye mete withal it shall be measured to you again. (Luke 6:38)

If thou return to the Almighty, thou shalt be built up, thou shalt put away iniquity far from thy tabernacles. Then shalt thou lay up gold as dust, and the gold of Ophir as the stones of the brooks. Yea, the Almighty shall be thy defence, and thou shalt have plenty of silver. For then shalt thou have thy delight in the Almighty, and shalt lift up thy face unto God. Thou shalt make thy prayer unto him, and he shall hear thee, and thou shalt pay thy vows. (Job 22:23–27)

Blessed is the man that walketh not in the counsel of the ungodly, nor standeth in the way of sinners, nor sitteth in the seat of the scornful. But his delight is in the law of the LORD; and in his law doth he meditate day and night. And he shall be like a tree planted by the rivers of water, that bringeth forth his fruit in his season; his leaf also shall not wither; and whatsoever he doeth shall prosper. The ungodly are not so: but are like the chaff which the wind driveth away. Therefore the ungodly shall not stand in the judgment, nor sinners in the congregation of the righteous. For the LORD knoweth the way of the righteous: but the way of the ungodly shall perish. (Psalm 1:1–6)

For I know the thoughts that I think toward you, saith the LORD, thoughts of peace, and not of evil, to give you an expected end. Then shall ye

> call upon me, and ye shall go and pray unto me, and I will hearken unto you. And ye shall seek me, and find me, when ye shall search for me with all your heart. And I will be found of you, saith the LORD: and I will turn away your captivity, and I will gather you from all the nations, and from all the places whither I have driven you, saith the LORD; and I will bring you again into the place whence I caused you to be carried away captive. (Jeremiah 29:11–14)

> And be not conformed to this world: but be ye transformed by the renewing of your mind, that ye may prove what is that good, and acceptable, and perfect, will of God. (Romans 12:2)

Conclusion
Trusting God

No matter our circumstances, trust God's promise that He's always with us, never giving us more than we can bear, even in the face of trials.

Understanding the Transformative Power of Divine Grace!

Understanding the transformative power of divine grace is crucial for several reasons:

1. *Personal transformation.* Divine grace has the ability to deeply impact individuals, bringing about inner transformation. It's through this grace that people can experience forgiveness, healing, and spiritual growth, enabling them to overcome personal struggles and become better versions of themselves.
2. *Spiritual connection.* Recognizing the power of divine grace fosters a deeper spiritual connection with the divine. It allows individuals to comprehend the unconditional love and mercy offered by a higher power, encouraging a more intimate relationship with the divine.
3. *Emotional and mental well-being.* Divine grace offers solace, peace, and reassurance. Understanding and accepting this grace can alleviate feelings of guilt, shame, or inadequacy, promoting emotional and mental well-being.
4. *Relationships and compassion.* Acknowledging the transformative nature of divine grace can also influence how individuals relate to others. It can inspire compassion, forgiveness, and empathy, fostering healthier and more understanding relationships.

5. *Hope and resilience.* Knowing that divine grace is transformative instills hope and resilience during challenging times. It provides the assurance that no matter the circumstances, there's a force of unconditional love available to support and uplift individuals.

Understanding the transformative power of divine grace brings personal growth, strengthens spiritual connections, enhances emotional well-being, influences relationships positively, and fosters hope and resilience in life's challenges.

The grace of God, as portrayed in the Bible, represents God's unmerited favor, love, and mercy toward humanity. Here's a deeper understanding of the grace of God according to the Bible:

1. *Unmerited favor.* Grace is often described as God's unmerited favor, which means that it is given freely and generously, not because of any merit or deserving action on the part of individuals. Ephesians 2:8–9 states, "For by grace you have been saved through faith. And this is not your own doing; it is the gift of God, not a result of works, so that no one may boast."
2. *Salvation and forgiveness.* The grace of God is closely tied to the concept of salvation and forgiveness. In the Bible, it is through God's grace that humanity is offered the opportunity for redemption and forgiveness of sins. Romans 3:24 explains, "And are justified by his grace as a gift, through the redemption that is in Christ Jesus."
3. *Gift of eternal life.* God's grace is often associated with the gift of eternal life. Believers are promised that through God's grace, they can have a restored relationship with Him and the hope of eternal life with Him (John 3:16).
4. *Sufficient in weakness.* The apostle Paul writes about the sufficiency of God's grace in times of weakness and difficulty. He notes in 2 Corinthians 12:9, "My grace is sufficient for you, for my power is made perfect in weakness."

This highlights that God's grace can strengthen and sustain believers during their trials.

5. *Transformative power*. The grace of God is not only about forgiveness but also about transformation. In Titus 2:11–12, God's grace teaches believers to live righteous and godly lives.
6. *Empowerment*. God's grace empowers believers to do good works and to walk in the paths of righteousness. It inspires acts of kindness, love, and service to others (Ephesians 2:10).
7. *No discrimination*. The grace of God is offered to all people, regardless of their background or past. It is inclusive and accessible to everyone who seeks it (Romans 10:12).
8. *Demonstration of God's love*. The grace of God is often viewed as a demonstration of God's great love for humanity. It is the basis for the covenantal relationship between God and His people.
9. *Eternal hope*. God's grace offers believers the assurance of eternal hope and a future in His presence, which is described in various passages, including Revelation 21.

God offers forgiveness, salvation, and blessings freely, not because we deserve them, but because of His love and mercy.

1. *Forgiveness and redemption*. God's grace offers forgiveness for our shortcomings and mistakes. It allows us to be redeemed, to start anew, no matter our past. This transformative aspect helps individuals move beyond guilt or shame and embrace a life guided by love and forgiveness.
2. *Transformation of character*. God's grace doesn't just pardon sins; it works within us to transform our character. It inspires us to become better individuals, encouraging qualities like love, compassion, patience, and kindness.
3. *Strength in weakness*. Grace helps us navigate life's challenges. It provides strength in times of weakness, giving

us the resilience to overcome obstacles and grow through adversity.

4. *Restoration of relationship.* God's grace restores our relationship with Him. It bridges the gap caused by our mistakes and allows us to have a meaningful connection with the divine, fostering a sense of belonging and purpose.
5. *Freedom and liberation.* Grace liberates us from the burden of trying to earn God's favor through our actions. It sets us free from the pressure of perfectionism and encourages us to live authentically, embracing our imperfections while striving to be better.

In essence, the transformative power of God's grace lies in its ability to change our hearts, minds, and lives. It brings healing, strength, and a profound sense of hope, guiding us toward a life filled with love, purpose, and spiritual growth.

Embracing God's Grace in Your Daily Life

The concept of God's grace is central to Christian faith and underscores the idea that God's love and mercy are freely given to those who believe and accept it. It is a source of comfort, assurance, and transformation in the lives of believers.

> But grow in grace, and in the knowledge of our Lord and Saviour Jesus Christ. To him be glory both now and for ever. Amen. (2 Peter 3:18 KJV)

God's Grace versus Human Efforts

Other religions emphasize earning salvation through good works, rituals, or becoming like gods, rooted in human pride. However, through Jesus Christ, we receive grace—a free gift, contrary to our prideful nature that believes we can achieve it ourselves.

Understanding God's Grace

As I learn and apply God's Word in my life, I grasp a deeper understanding of His will. Everything—my past, present, and future—is a result of God's amazing grace. Every failure humbles me, increasing my dependence on God's grace and allowing Jesus to take precedence in my life.

God's Grace in Action

The passage in Ephesians 2:1–10 highlights God's mercy and love. Even when we were spiritually dead, God, in His grace, revived us through Christ. Our salvation isn't by our efforts but by God's gift through faith.

Accepting God's Grace

Recognizing our unworthiness is the first step to receiving God's grace. Pride precedes downfall, but humility brings honor. Those striving to earn their way to God insult His grace and operate in pride, which opposes love.

Embracing God's Compassion

God's essence is love and compassion. He orchestrates our failures to showcase His immense grace. The cross demonstrates His unconditional love, paying for our sins, past and present.

Transformed by the Holy Spirit

The Holy Spirit guides us in truth and obedience, molding our desires toward love and obedience to God. We're incapable of obedience through our efforts; it's the Holy Spirit's work within us that enables us to love and obey.

Living in Gratitude and Resting in Grace

Our relationship with God is about abiding in Him, similar to a branch in a tree. Our role is to remain in Christ, allowing the Holy Spirit to produce fruits of love, joy, and more. Love is the core fruit that draws others to God.

Finding Strength in Weakness

Our failures only magnify God's grace. Our weaknesses become avenues for God's strength and compassion to manifest. Trusting in His grace glorifies God more than claiming our own achievements.

Seeking Transformation through Prayer

Pray for a supernatural encounter with God's presence. Allow the Holy Spirit to transform your heart, empowering you to love and touch others. God eagerly responds to such prayers from His children.

Understanding the Will of God!

Understanding the will of God holds significant importance for several reasons:

1. *Guidance and direction.* Recognizing God's will helps individuals navigate life's decisions. It provides a moral compass, offering guidance and direction in making choices that align with higher principles.
2. *Spiritual connection.* Understanding God's will fosters a deeper spiritual connection. It allows individuals to seek closeness with the divine, facilitating a stronger relationship and a sense of purpose.
3. *Personal fulfillment.* Knowing and following God's will often leads to personal fulfillment. It can bring a sense of contentment and satisfaction as one aligns their life with a higher purpose beyond personal desires.
4. *Clarity in decision-making.* Recognizing God's will offers clarity in decision-making processes. It helps individuals discern between right and wrong, especially in morally complex situations.
5. *Peace and trust.* Understanding God's will instills peace and trust. It reassures individuals that there's a divine plan, even in uncertain times, fostering a sense of security and hope.
6. *Living with intention.* Knowing God's will encourages intentional living. It motivates individuals to live in a way that reflects their beliefs and values, contributing positively to themselves and their communities.

In essence, understanding the will of God provides guidance, strengthens spiritual connections, fosters personal fulfillment, aids decision-making, brings peace and trust, and encourages intentional living in alignment with higher principles.

Here are some key points to help you understand more regarding the concept of God's will according to the Bible:

1. *God's sovereignty.* The Bible teaches that God is sovereign over all creation. His will is supreme, and He has ultimate authority and control over the universe (Isaiah 46:10; Ephesians 1:11).
2. *God's moral will.* The Bible contains many commandments, principles, and moral guidelines that reflect God's will for human behavior. These include the Ten Commandments and various ethical teachings found in both the Old and New Testaments.
3. *God's redemptive will.* A significant aspect of God's will is His redemptive plan for humanity. This plan is fulfilled through the life, death, and resurrection of Jesus Christ, offering salvation and reconciliation to all who believe (John 6:40; 1 Timothy 2:3–4).
4. *God's providential will.* The Bible teaches that God is actively involved in the world's events and that His providential will guides the course of history. This includes His plans for nations, rulers, and individuals (Proverbs 19:21; Romans 13:1).
5. *Discerning God's will.* Believers are encouraged to seek and discern God's will for their lives. This may involve prayer, seeking guidance from the Holy Spirit, and studying the Scriptures to make wise and righteous choices (Proverbs 3:5–6; Romans 12:2).
6. *Surrender to God's will.* A key aspect of Christian faith is surrendering to God's will, acknowledging that His plans are ultimately for the best. This can involve yielding one's own desires and submitting to God's guidance (Matthew 6:10; Luke 22:42).

7. *God's individual plans.* While there are universal aspects of God's will, there is also room for individual paths and callings. God may have specific plans for each person's life, which can include vocations, missions, and service to others (Jeremiah 29:11; Ephesians 2:10).
8. *Walk in obedience.* Obedience to God's will is highly emphasized in the Bible. Believers are called to live in accordance with His commands and ethical principles, reflecting His character (Micah 6:8; Colossians 1:9–10).
9. *Trust and faith.* Understanding and following God's will often requires trust and faith in His wisdom and goodness. Believers trust that God's plans are ultimately for their benefit and the fulfillment of His purposes (Hebrews 11:6; Romans 8:28).

Discovering God's Will

Every Christian wants to know God's plan for their life. But what exactly is God's will, and how do we find it? Is it hidden or obvious? Can we mess things up by making the wrong choices?

God's Will Revealed

The good news is we can know and live out God's will through prayer, Scripture, and the Holy Spirit. God doesn't want us to spend our lives trying to figure Him out like a puzzle. When we seek Him, He reveals Himself to us.

Understanding God's Will

While we can't fully understand God's will, He guides us through prayer and Scripture. He wants us to know how to please Him and has given us ways to align ourselves with His will.

What is "the Will of God"?

Jesus taught us to pray for God's will to be done (Matthew 6:10). God's will aligns with His plan and purpose. For example, He desires salvation for every one (2 Peter 3:9) and reveals His will to those who seek Him.

God's Will in Action

Throughout history, God revealed His will to people like Noah and Moses. They adjusted their lives to follow God's plan, believing, obeying, and experiencing God's work through them.

Understanding God's Will Today

When we speak of God's will, it's about seeking His guidance in significant decisions like marriage, work, and where we live. But God's will isn't a mystery; it's about being humble, merciful, and just (Micah 6:8).

God's Will versus Our Desires

God's will might not match our plans. Jesus's prayer before His crucifixion showed submission to God's will despite His human desire to avoid suffering (Matthew 26:39). Jesus set aside His will to embrace God's eternal work.

Listed below are ten verses and passages that can help us understand God's will and how it is at work within us:

> And this is the will of him who sent me, that I shall lose none of all those he has given me, but raise them up at the last day. For my Father's will is that everyone who looks to the Son and believes in him shall have eternal life, and I will raise them up at the last day. (John 6:39–40)

Give thanks in all circumstances; for this is God's will for you in Christ Jesus. (1 Thessalonians 5:18)

It is God's will that you should be sanctified: that you should avoid sexual immorality; that each of you should learn to control your own body in a way that is holy and honorable, not in passionate lust like the pagans, who do not know God. (1 Thessalonians 4:3–5)

This is good, and pleases God our Savior, who wants all people to be saved and to come to a knowledge of the truth. (1 Timothy 2:3–4)

All the peoples of the earth are regarded as nothing. He does as he pleases with the powers of heaven and the peoples of the earth. No one can hold back his hand or say to him: "What have you done?" (Daniel 4:35)

Grace and peace to you from God *our Father* and the Lord Jesus Christ, who gave himself for our sins to rescue us from the present evil age, according to the will of our God and Father. (Galatians 1:3–4)

The people there pleaded with Paul not to go up to Jerusalem. Then Paul answered, "Why are you weeping and breaking my heart? I am ready not only to be bound, but also to die in Jerusalem for the name of the Lord Jesus." When he would not be dissuaded, we gave up and said, 'The Lord's will be done. (Acts 21:12–14)

> Therefore God has mercy on whom he wants to have mercy, and he hardens whom he wants to harden. One of you will say to me: "Then why does God still blame us? For who is able to resist his will?" But who are you, a human being, to talk back to God? "Shall what is formed say to the one who formed it, 'Why did you make me like this?'" Does not the potter have the right to make out of the same lump of clay some pottery for special purposes and some for common use? (Romans 9:18–23)

> Obey them not only to win their favor when their eye is on you, but as slaves of Christ, doing the will of God from your heart. (Ephesians 6:6)

> Why, you do not even know what will happen tomorrow. What is your life? You are a mist that appears for a little while and then vanishes. Instead, you ought to say, "If it is the Lord's will, we will live and do this or that." (James 4:14–15)

As you meditate on these Scriptures, pray that God will draw you close to Him and reveal His will as you seek Him.

Understanding God's Will

Discovering God's will for our lives is possible. To hear His voice, we need to seek Him earnestly, get to know Him better, and grow our relationship with Him because of who He is. Praying for God to teach us His will is crucial, just like the Psalmist did (Psalm 143:10).

Living According to God's Will

Jesus emphasized that by seeking God and living by His Word, we align ourselves with God's will. Those who do God's will become part of His family (Mark 3:35).

Differentiating God's Will from the World

Sometimes things that seem good aren't aligned with God's will. Paul understood God's will for his life, like becoming an Apostle (1 Corinthians 1:1). He taught that transforming our minds helps us know God's perfect will (Romans 12:2).

Discovering God's Plan Vital Keys

Discovering God's plan requires some vital steps:

1. *Walking with God.* Developing a relationship with God through His Word, prayer, and church involvement.
2. *Surrendering to God's will.* Being willing to do whatever God desires.
3. *Obeying what we know.* Obeying what God has already revealed in His Word.
4. *Seeking godly advice.* Seeking input from wise, God-fearing mentors.
5. *Recognizing our gifts.* Understanding how God has uniquely gifted us.
6. *Listening to God.* Learning to listen to God during prayer.
7. *Listening to your heart.* When walking with the Lord, our desires align with God's plan.

God's will is that we give thanks in everything (1 Thessalonians 5:18). What an incredible challenge it is to abide by the truth of this verse! Yet, because the Lord's commandments are not grievous (1 John 5:3), we can even be thankful in the midst of great difficulty.

I heard the following twenty-three encouraging reasons to be thankful from BBN Global radio, which touched my heart. Here, I quote:

1. God cares for me (1 Peter 5:7).
2. God's forgiveness is available (Psalms 103:8–12).

3. God faithfully guides (Psalms 48:14)
4. Being part of a biblical local church (Acts 2:42–47).
5. God is good (Romans 2:4).
6. God gives us eternal life (John 3:16).
7. God never changes (James 1:17).
8. God's perfect timing (Ecclesiastes 3:11).
9. God's help is enough for everything (2 Corinthians 9:8).
10. God strengthens me (Philippians 4:13).
11. God answers my prayer (James 5:16–18).
12. God's constant presence (Psalms 139:7–10)
13. The Holy Spirit always helps me (John 14:26).
14. God's patience with us (2 Peter 3:9).
15. A good biblical marriage (Mark 10:9).
16. I hear Jesus voice (John 10:27).
17. A godly pastor (Ephesians 4:11).
18. Sufficient grace always (2 Corinthians 9:8).
19. Children following Christ (3 John 4).
20. God gives us clarity of mind (2 Timothy 1:7).
21. God's plan for me (Jeremiah 29:11).
22. This day God made (Psalms 118:24).
23. God's bountiful provision (Philippians 4:19).

Following these steps helps us align ourselves with God's will and experience the fulfilling adventure He has planned for us.

Understanding the Peace of God!

Understanding the peace of God holds immense significance for various aspects of life:

1. *Emotional well-being.* Knowing and embracing God's peace can bring emotional stability. It offers a sense of calmness, reducing anxiety, stress, and worry in challenging situations.
2. *Spiritual connection.* Understanding God's peace deepens one's spiritual connection. It fosters trust and reliance on a higher power, promoting inner tranquility amid life's uncertainties.
3. *Conflict resolution.* The peace of God guides individuals in resolving conflicts. It encourages patience, forgiveness, and empathy, fostering harmonious relationships.
4. *Strength in adversity.* Embracing God's peace provides strength during difficult times. It offers comfort and resilience, enabling individuals to endure hardships with a sense of hope and courage.
5. *Decision-making.* Awareness of God's peace aids in decision-making. It promotes clarity of mind, allowing for wise choices based on peace rather than fear or haste.
6. *Overall well-being.* Understanding and experiencing God's peace contributes to overall well-being. It nurtures a positive outlook on life, encouraging gratitude, contentment, and a sense of purpose.

Ultimately, understanding the peace of God impacts emotional stability, fosters spiritual connection, aids conflict resolution, provides strength in adversity, aids decision-making, and contributes to overall well-being, allowing individuals to live more fulfilling and peaceful lives.

Here are some key points to help you comprehend more regarding the concept of the peace of God according to the Bible:

1. *God's character as a source of peace.* God is the ultimate source of peace. His nature is one of love, goodness, and tranquility, and believers are encouraged to seek and experience this peace through a relationship with Him (Philippians 4:7; Isaiah 26:3).
2. *Peace with God through Jesus Christ.* The Bible teaches that reconciliation with God is made possible through faith in Jesus Christ. Believers are said to have peace with God, as the barrier of sin is removed, and they are justified through Christ's sacrifice (Romans 5:1; Ephesians 2:14–16).
3. *Inner peace.* The peace of God extends to the inner peace that believers can experience. It is described as a sense of calm, contentment, and assurance, even in the midst of life's challenges (John 14:27; Philippians 4:6–7).
4. *Freedom from anxiety and fear.* The peace of God is associated with freedom from anxiety, fear, and worry. Believers are encouraged to cast their cares upon God and trust in His care (1 Peter 5:7; Philippians 4:6–7).
5. *Conflict resolution.* The peace of God is often linked to resolving conflicts and promoting harmony among individuals and communities. Believers are urged to be peacemakers and seek reconciliation with others (Matthew 5:9; Romans 12:18).
6. *Trust in God's providence.* Understanding the peace of God also involves trusting in God's providence and His sovereign control over all circumstances. Believers are encouraged to acknowledge that God's plans are for their good

and that they can have confidence in His care (Proverbs 3:5–6; Romans 8:28).

7. *Shalom.* The Hebrew word "shalom" is often used in the Bible to describe peace. Shalom represents not just the absence of conflict but a state of wholeness, completeness, and well-being. It encompasses physical, emotional, and spiritual harmony.
8. *Fruit of the Spirit.* The peace of God is one of the "Fruit of the Spirit" listed in Galatians 5:22–23. This indicates that it is a characteristic of a person who is led by the Holy Spirit and seeks to live in accordance with God's will.
9. *Eternal peace.* Believers are promised the hope of eternal peace in God's presence, where there will be no more sorrow, pain, or conflict (Revelation 21:4).

Finding Peace by Following God

The Bible says, "Walk according to the Spirit, not the flesh" (Romans 8:4).

Why Distractions Matter

Like how distracted driving causes accidents, distractions harm our connection with God. Focusing on worldly desires brings death, but focusing on spiritual things brings life and peace (Romans 8:6).

Walking with God's Spirit

Following God's guidance, though we can't do it perfectly (Galatians 5:16), leads to life. However, living for selfish desires leads to spiritual death.

Choosing Spiritual over Selfish Desires

Focusing on selfish desires results in spiritual death. Most things the world promotes distance us from God (Romans 8:7–8).

Living by God's Spirit

For life and peace, prioritize spiritual activities and let God guide your thoughts and actions (Galatians 6:7–8).

Understanding God's Peace
The Bible's Gift

The peace of God brings inner tranquility, reconciliation with God, and harmonious relationships.

Meaning of God's Peace

God's peace isn't like worldly peace, tied to circumstances. It exists even amid chaos, guarding your heart and mind (Philippians 4:7).

God's Peace Protects

It acts as a shield against anxiety and fear, keeping you calm and focused (Philippians 4:7).

God's Peace Is Ever-Present

God's peace should dwell within you all the time, being a refuge in life's challenges (2 Thessalonians 3:16).

Experiencing God's Peace in Your Heart

What's in your heart shows through your words and actions. When God's peace rules in your heart, it affects how you react to situations.

How to Obtain God's Peace

Prayer is key. Don't let worries take over; instead, present your concerns to God (Philippians 4:6). Exchange your worries for God's peace.

Finding Peace in the Bible

The Bible is full of verses offering peace during good and tough times, revealing Jesus as the Prince of Peace.

Bible Verses about Peace

Verses like John 16:33 and Ephesians 3:18 show Jesus's promise of peace.

Peace in Hard Times

In tough moments, prayer brings peace (Philippians 4:6–7). The discipline of hardships brings righteousness and peace (Hebrews 12:11).

Peace with Others

Living in peace with others is crucial. Peacemakers are blessed (Matthew 5:9).

Blessings of Peace

God's peace, coupled with love and faith, is a gift from God and Jesus (Ephesians 6:23).

Here's how to understand "peace with God" according to the Bible:

1. *Reconciliation through Christ.* Peace with God refers to the restoration of a right relationship between human beings and God. According to the Bible, all humans are born with a separation from God due to sin (Romans 3:23). Through the sacrifice of Jesus Christ on the cross, God offers a way for people to be reconciled with Him (Romans 5:1).
2. *Justification.* Believers are declared righteous and justified by God through faith in Jesus Christ. This justification is

a key aspect of achieving peace with God. It means that believers are no longer seen as guilty before God but are instead counted as righteous because of Christ's atonement (Romans 5:9).

3. *Freedom from God's wrath.* Prior to reconciliation, the Bible speaks of humanity as being under God's wrath due to sin. Peace with God means being liberated from this state of condemnation and punishment (Romans 5:9).
4. *Access to God.* Through peace with God, believers gain access to God the Father. They can approach God in prayer and relationship, knowing that they are no longer separated by sin (Ephesians 2:18).
5. *Grace and faith.* Peace with God is made possible by God's grace and is received through faith. It is not something that can be earned through good works but is a gift from God (Ephesians 2:8–9).
6. *Reconciliation for all.* The message of peace with God is not limited to a select few but is offered to all people. It is a universal invitation to come into the right relationship with God (John 3:16; 2 Corinthians 5:19).
7. *Inner peace.* While "peace with God" primarily refers to reconciliation, it can also lead to a sense of inner peace and well-being for believers. This inner peace comes from knowing that one is in a harmonious relationship with the Creator (Philippians 4:7).

Understanding "peace with God" is central to the Christian faith, as it represents the hope of salvation, the assurance of forgiveness, and the restoration of a loving relationship between humans and their Creator. It is a foundational concept in the New Testament, and it brings comfort and a sense of reconciliation to believers.

Understanding and Adopting God's Vision

Understanding and adopting God's vision is important for several reasons:

1. *Purpose and direction.* God's vision offers a sense of purpose and direction in life. It guides individuals toward meaningful goals and aspirations aligned with God's greater plan.
2. *Alignment with divine will.* Embracing God's vision ensures alignment with His will. It allows individuals to live in accordance with the principles of love, compassion, justice, and righteousness.
3. *Personal growth and transformation.* God's vision often challenges individuals to grow and transform. It encourages spiritual, emotional, and moral development, fostering character strengths and virtues.
4. *Impact and service.* God's vision often involves serving others and making a positive impact in the world. Adopting His vision encourages selflessness, generosity, and a desire to contribute to the well-being of others.
5. *Faith and trust.* Embracing God's vision requires faith and trust in His plan. It nurtures a deeper relationship with God, fostering reliance on His guidance and providence.
6. *Fulfillment and contentment.* Living according to God's vision can bring a sense of fulfillment and contentment.

It leads to a life that's meaningful, purpose-driven, and in harmony with divine principles.

Ultimately, understanding and adopting God's vision provides purpose, alignment with divine will, personal growth, impact and service to others, faith and trust, as well as fulfillment and contentment in life.

In the Bible, the concept of "God's vision" is not explicitly stated as a singular term, but it can be understood by examining various aspects of God's purpose, plans, and desires as described in the Scriptures. Here's how to understand God's vision based on the Bible:

1. *Creation and order*. The Bible begins with the creation account in Genesis, where God's vision is to bring order out of chaos and to create a harmonious world. God's vision is to establish a well-ordered and good creation where everything has its place and purpose (Genesis 1:31).
2. *Covenant and relationship*. Throughout the Bible, God establishes covenants with humanity, such as the Abrahamic, Mosaic, and new covenants. These covenants reflect God's vision for a relationship with His people, where He promises to be their God, and they promise to be His people (Jeremiah 31:33).
3. *Redemption and salvation*. A significant part of God's vision is the redemption and salvation of humanity. The Bible unfolds the narrative of God's plan to offer forgiveness and reconciliation through Jesus Christ, reflecting God's desire to bring people back into a right relationship with Him (John 3:16; Ephesians 1:7).
4. *Justice and righteousness*. God's vision includes a call for justice and righteousness. The Bible emphasizes God's concern for the well-being of the marginalized, the oppressed, and the vulnerable. His vision includes a just and righteous society where people are treated with fairness and compassion (Isaiah 1:17; Micah 6:8).

5. *Kingdom of God.* Jesus often spoke about the "kingdom of God" or the "kingdom of heaven." This represents God's vision for a kingdom where His rule and reign are established on earth, bringing about peace, love, and the fulfillment of His purposes (Matthew 6:10; Luke 17:21).
6. *Transformation and renewal.* God's vision also includes the transformation and renewal of individuals and communities. Believers are encouraged to be conformed to the image of Christ, reflecting God's vision of a transformed and renewed life (Romans 12:2; 2 Corinthians 5:17).
7. *Eternal life.* God's vision extends to the promise of eternal life for believers. The Bible speaks of the vision of believers dwelling with God in His presence for all eternity, free from suffering and sorrow (Revelation 21:3–4).
8. *The glory of God.* Ultimately, God's vision is for His glory to be revealed and acknowledged throughout creation. His vision is that all of creation would ultimately worship and glorify Him (Isaiah 43:7; Revelation 5:13).

God's vision, as portrayed in the Bible, is expansive and encompasses themes of creation, relationship, redemption, justice, transformation, and eternity. It reflects His overarching purpose and plan for humanity and all of creation. Understanding this vision can provide a profound sense of purpose and direction for believers.

God's Vision for us, or…

> Where there is no vision, the people perish.
> (Proverbs 29:18 KJV)

Why does the Bible say vision is so important in your life?

Because *"where there is no vision, the people perish"* (Proverbs 29:18 KJV). Here are three reasons why it's essential to have a clear vision of God's purpose for your life.

Without God's vision, there's indecisiveness. James 1:8 GW says, *"A person who has doubts is thinking about two different things at the same time and can't make up his mind about anything."*

Without God's vision for your future, you drift and wander through life. You don't have goals, purpose, or meaning. When you just let life happen to you, you're not really living!

With no vision, you waste time, and you miss opportunities. You don't make the most of what you've been given, and that makes you a poor steward of your life. You end up just cruising. And when you're cruising, you're always heading downhill.

Without God's vision, there's division. If you don't understand God's vision for your life, how can you expect others to support you in your purpose? In fact, the lack of vision makes you vulnerable to others, steering you toward what they think or assume your purpose is.

Only God can tell you your purpose because he created you specifically and uniquely to live it out. And only following his vision will allow you to live the *abundant life* God intends for you. If you aren't sure where you're headed, then don't expect anybody else to go with you.

Proverbs 28:2 says,

> When the country is in chaos, everybody has a plan to fix it—But it takes a leader of real understanding to straighten things out. (The Message)

Vision is the antidote to division.

Without God's vision, there's collision. For many people, life is just a series of relational confrontations, financial crashes, and personal crises. It's like a bumper car ride, where you just keep getting hit from all sides. Without God's clear direction for your life, you will inevitably hit a dead end.

The Bible tells us that not following God's vision can lead to losing faith, just like a wrecked ship (1 Timothy 1:19 GW).

Discovering God's plan for our lives needs prayer, thinking, and listening to God. It's about seeing things clearly with faith, not fear. When faith guides us, we understand our purpose better.

God has a special plan for each of us, aiming to show His glory through our lives. His vision isn't like our plans; we want all answers upfront, but God reveals His plan gradually when we're ready.

As we follow God, He equips us for His purposes. Even amid challenges, we trust His plan will succeed.

In life, we set goals—big or small. Yet, the ultimate goal is understanding Jesus's teaching: to seek God's Kingdom and righteousness.

This Kingdom is God's vision for the world and us. It's about love, healing, and living like Jesus. Knowing God's love is crucial—we are deeply loved by Him more than anything else.

Jesus points to nature to show how much God cares. If He cares for birds and flowers, how much more does He care for us? So worry less about daily needs and focus on God.

Life can get overwhelming with responsibilities, but finding peace comes from God alone. Trusting in Him gives tranquility and hope.

Seeking God's kingdom and His righteousness means not worrying about the future. God's plan surpasses our worries and fears.

Jesus invites us to make God the center of our lives. Trusting His plan over our own, we experience His immense love and receive everything we need.

God's vision is for us to become like Christ. Let's pray to trust His vision over our plans, in Jesus's name. Amen.

Understanding Life according to God

Understanding life according to God is important for various reasons:

1. *Guidance and direction.* God offers guidance and direction through His teachings and principles outlined in sacred texts. Understanding life through God's perspective provides a moral and ethical compass for decision-making and living purposefully.
2. *Meaning and purpose.* God's perspective on life often includes a deeper sense of meaning and purpose. Recognizing His plan for individuals' lives can bring clarity and fulfillment in pursuing their unique calling.
3. *Morality and ethics.* God's perspective establishes a framework of morality and ethics, guiding individuals to distinguish between right and wrong. It fosters a life based on values such as love, compassion, justice, and forgiveness.
4. *Relationships.* Understanding life according to God helps in building healthier relationships. It emphasizes love, empathy, and forgiveness, nurturing stronger connections with others.
5. *Peace and contentment.* Embracing God's perspective often leads to inner peace and contentment. Trusting in His plan can alleviate anxiety and bring a sense of serenity amid life's uncertainties.

6. *Eternal perspective.* God's perspective extends beyond this life, offering an eternal perspective. It encourages individuals to focus on spiritual growth and prepare for life beyond the earthly realm.
7. *Community and service.* It motivates individuals to serve and contribute positively to their communities. Understanding life through God's perspective often involves selflessness and compassion toward others.

Understanding life according to God provides guidance, purpose, moral values, better relationships, inner peace, an eternal perspective, and a call to serve others, contributing to a more fulfilling and meaningful existence.

The good life. What does it mean to you? Is it about spending time with loved ones, living fully, and being generous? Or is it a constant chase for more—more money, possessions, and influence? Our world bombards us with messages about what a good life should look like—often revolving around material wealth, success, and appearances. But these messages never seem to be enough, always leaving us thirsty for more.

Studies consistently show that having more doesn't necessarily make us happier. Thanksgiving becomes a time to reflect on what true happiness is really about. The idea of a good life differs from person to person—for some, it's about possessions and success while, for others, it's about simplicity, meaningful connections, or making a positive impact.

Despite what the world tells us, Jesus challenges this notion. In a parable, he speaks of a man with an abundance who selfishly hoards his wealth, failing to consider God or the needs of others. Jesus highlights greed and fear as underlying issues when we chase after more rather than trusting in God's abundance and living generously.

Contrary to the world's message of accumulation, Jesus offers a different path to the good life—one centered on giving rather than gaining. He urges us not to worry about material needs but to seek God's kingdom first. The key to the Good Life, according to Jesus, lies in being rich toward God and others, embracing generosity, and trust in God's provision.

Living a fulfilling life, according to Jesus, isn't about chasing after temporary pleasures but finding contentment in God's provision and living generously. It's about prioritizing a life of faith, trust, and generosity rather than the pursuit of material possessions or success.

Finding the Good Life means being rich toward God and acknowledging and embracing God's generosity toward us. Jesus assures us that living generously is the pathway to a rewarding and abundant life, focusing not on hoarding but on giving and trusting in God's provision.

The Good Life, as Jesus teaches, isn't found in materialism but in a life of trust, generosity, and faith in God's abundant provision.

Here are a few selected Bible verses regarding living a good life

The Lord shall preserve thee from all evil: he shall preserve thy soul. The Lord shall preserve thy going out and thy coming in from this time forth, and even for evermore.

> See then that ye walk circumspectly, not as fools, but as wise, Redeeming the time, because the days are evil. (Psalm 121:7–8)

> As in water face answereth to face, so the heart of man to man. (Ephesians 5:15–16)

> For we walk by faith, not by sight. (Proverbs 27:19)

> And whatsoever ye do, do it heartily, as to the Lord, and not unto men; Knowing that of the Lord ye shall receive the reward of the inheritance: for ye serve the Lord Christ. (2 Corinthians 5:7)

He that followeth after righteousness and mercy findeth life, righteousness, and honour. (Colossians 3:23–24)

For what shall it profit a man, if he shall gain the whole world, and lose his own soul? (Proverbs 21:21)

My flesh and my heart faileth: but God is the strength of my heart, and my portion forever. (Mark 8:36)

For he that will love life, and see good days, let him refrain his tongue from evil, and his lips that they speak no guile: Let him eschew evil, and do good; let him seek peace, and ensue it. (Psalm 73:26)

To everything there is a season, and a time to every purpose under the heaven. (1 Peter 3:10–11)

For thou art my rock and my fortress; therefore for thy name's sake lead me and guide me. (Ecclesiastes 3:1)

Keep thy heart with all diligence; for out of it are the issues of life. (Psalm 31:3)

Shew me thy ways, O Lord; teach me thy paths. (Proverbs 4:23)

And be not conformed to this world: but be ye transformed by the renewing of your mind, that ye may prove what is that good, and acceptable, and perfect, will of God. (Psalm 25:4)

> And Jesus said unto them, I am the bread of life: he that cometh to me shall never hunger; and he that believeth on me shall never thirst. (Romans 12:2)

> Rest in the Lord and wait patiently for him: fret not thyself because of him who prospereth in his way, because of the man who bringeth wicked devices to pass. (John 6:35)

> Surely goodness and mercy shall follow me all the days of my life: and I will dwell in the house of the Lord forever. (Psalm 37:7)

> He that keepeth his mouth keepeth his life: but he that openeth wide his lips shall have destruction. (Psalm 23:6)

> In that I command thee this day to love the Lord thy God, to walk in his ways, and to keep his commandments and his statutes and his judgments, that thou mayest live and multiply: and the Lord thy God shall bless thee in the land whither thou goest to possess it. (Proverbs 13:3)

Understanding life according to the Bible involves considering the biblical perspective on the nature, purpose, and significance of human existence. Here are key aspects to help you comprehend life according to the Bible:

1. *Creation by God.* The Bible teaches that life originates from God, who is the Creator of all living things. In the creation account in Genesis, God forms humanity from the dust of the earth and breathes life into them (Genesis 2:7).
2. *Image of God.* According to the Bible, human beings are created in the image of God. This concept underscores the

inherent dignity and value of every individual. It implies a reflection of God's attributes, such as reason, morality, and creativity (Genesis 1:27).

3. *Purpose and meaning.* The Bible emphasizes that life has a purpose and meaning. The ultimate purpose is to know, love, and serve God, living in accordance with His moral and ethical principles. This relationship with God gives significance to human existence (Ecclesiastes 12:13).
4. *Moral choices.* The Bible teaches that life involves making moral choices. The Scriptures provide guidance on how to make choices that align with God's will and lead to righteousness (Proverbs 3:5–6).
5. *Fall and sin.* The Bible acknowledges that humanity has fallen into sin and is separated from God. This condition is a result of disobedience and rebellion. Redemption and reconciliation with God are central themes of the Bible (Romans 3:23; Romans 6:23).
6. *Salvation and eternal life.* The Bible offers the hope of salvation and eternal life through faith in Jesus Christ. Believers are promised forgiveness of sins and the gift of eternal life with God (John 3:16; Romans 6:23).
7. *Transformation and renewal.* The Bible teaches that believers can experience transformation and renewal through the indwelling of the Holy Spirit. This involves becoming more Christlike in character (Romans 12:2; 2 Corinthians 5:17).
8. *Relationships and love.* Life, as described in the Bible, involves meaningful relationships with others. Love, compassion, and care for one another are emphasized as integral aspects of living out one's faith (Matthew 22:39; 1 Corinthians 13:4–7).
9. *Service and witness.* Believers are encouraged to serve others and be witnesses of their faith. Living a life of service, sharing the gospel, and demonstrating God's love are important expressions of the Christian life (Matthew 5:16; Acts 1:8).
10. *Eternal hope.* The Bible points to the hope of an eternal life with God in His presence, free from suffering and sorrow.

It speaks of the promise of a new heaven and a new earth (Revelation 21:3–4).

Understanding life according to the Bible involves recognizing its divine origin, purpose, moral choices, the impact of sin, the promise of salvation, transformation, relationships, service, and the eternal hope offered to believers. It is a multifaceted view of life that provides guidance and meaning to those who follow its teachings.

Now I'm going to talk to you about the most important thing you will ever have.

First, from the beginning, man has been gifted by God with the fundamental right to choose between good and evil. And second, that we were made in God's own image and, therefore, we are expected to use all our own power of thought and judgment in exercising that choice; and further, that if we open our hearts to God, He has promised to work within us.

Did you know that no document in world history has changed the world for the better, as did the Ten Commandments?

Western civilization—the civilization that developed universal human rights, created women's equality, ended slavery, created parliamentary democracy, among other unique achievements—would not have developed without them.

As you will see when each of the Ten Commandments is explained, these commandments are as relevant today as when they were given over three thousand years ago. In fact, they're so relevant that the Ten Commandments are all that is necessary to make a good world, a world free of tyranny and cruelty.

Imagine for a moment a world in which there was no murder or theft. In such a world, there would be no need for armies, police, or weapons. Men, women, and children could walk anywhere, at any time of day or night, without any fear of being killed or robbed.

Imagine further a world in which no one coveted what belonged to their neighbor, a world in which children honored their mother and father, and the family unit thrived, a world in which people obeyed the injunction not to lie.

The recipe for a good world is all there—in these ten sublime commandments. But there is a catch. The Ten Commandments are predicated on the belief that they were given by an Authority higher than any man, any king, or any government. That's why the sentence preceding the Ten Commandments asserts the following: "God spoke all these words."

You see, if the Ten Commandments, as great as they are, were given by any human authority, then any person could say: "Who is this man Moses? Who is this king or queen? Who is this government to tell me how I should behave? Okay, so why is God indispensable to the Ten Commandments?

Because, to put it as directly as possible, if it isn't God who declares murder wrong, murder isn't wrong. Yes, this strikes many people today as incomprehensible, even absurd. Many of you are thinking, "Is this guy saying you can't be a good person if you don't believe in God?" Let me respond as clearly as possible: I am not saying that. Of course, there are good people who don't believe in God, just as there are bad people who do. And many of you are also thinking, "I believe murder is wrong. I don't need God to tell me." Now that response is only half true. I have no doubt that if you're an atheist and you say you believe murder is wrong, you believe murder is wrong. But forgive me. You do need God to tell you. We all need God to tell us. You see, even if you figured out murder is wrong on your own, without God and the Ten Commandments, how do you know it's wrong? Do not believe it's wrong. I mean, know it's wrong? The fact is that you can't. Because without God, right and wrong are just personal beliefs. Personal opinions. I think shoplifting is okay; you don't. Unless there is a God, all morality is just opinion and belief. And virtually every atheist philosopher has acknowledged this.

Another problem with the view that you don't need God to believe that murder is wrong is that a lot of people haven't shared your view. And you don't have to go back very far in history to prove this. In the twentieth century, millions of people in Communist societies and under Nazism killed about one hundred million people—

and that doesn't count a single soldier killed in war. So don't get too confident about people's ability to figure out right from wrong without a Higher Authority.

It's all too easy to be swayed by a government or a demagogue or an ideology or to rationalize that the wrong you are doing isn't really wrong. And even if you do figure out what is right and wrong, God is still necessary.

People who know the difference between right and wrong do the wrong thing all the time. You know why? Because they can. They can because they think no one is watching. But if you recognize that God is the source of moral law, you believe that He is always watching. So even if you're an atheist, you would want people to live by the moral laws of the Ten Commandments. And even an atheist has to admit that the more people who believe God gave them—and therefore, they are not just opinions—the better the world would be.

In three thousand years, no one has ever come up with a better system than the God-based Ten Commandments for making a better world. And no one ever will (*The Ten Commandments: Still the Best Moral Code* by Dennis Prager).

Understanding What Matters Most in Life

Understanding life according to God is important for various reasons:

1. *Guidance and direction.* God offers guidance and direction through His teachings and principles outlined in sacred texts. Understanding life through God's perspective provides a moral and ethical compass for decision-making and living purposefully.
2. *Meaning and purpose.* God's perspective on life often includes a deeper sense of meaning and purpose. Recognizing His plan for individuals' lives can bring clarity and fulfillment in pursuing their unique calling.
3. *Morality and ethics.* God's perspective establishes a framework of morality and ethics, guiding individuals to distinguish between right and wrong. It fosters a life based on values such as love, compassion, justice, and forgiveness.
4. *Relationships.* Understanding life according to God helps in building healthier relationships. It emphasizes love, empathy, and forgiveness, nurturing stronger connections with others.
5. Peace and Contentment: Embracing God's perspective often leads to inner peace and contentment. Trusting in His plan can alleviate anxiety and bring a sense of serenity amid life's uncertainties.

6. *Eternal perspective.* God's perspective extends beyond this life, offering an eternal perspective. It encourages individuals to focus on spiritual growth and prepare for life beyond the earthly realm.
7. *Community and service.* It motivates individuals to serve and contribute positively to their communities. Understanding life through God's perspective often involves selflessness and compassion toward others.

Understanding life according to God provides guidance, purpose, moral values, better relationships, inner peace, an eternal perspective, and a call to serve others, contributing to a more fulfilling and meaningful existence.

While the Bible contains many teachings and guidance, here are some of the central aspects of what matters most in life according to Scripture:

1. *Love.* Love is emphasized as one of the most important principles in the Bible. The Bible teaches that loving God and loving one's neighbor are the greatest commandments (Matthew 22:37–40). Love is seen as the foundation for all other virtues, for God is love (1 John 4:16)
2. *Faith.* Faith in God is a core element of the Christian life. Believing in God and having faith in His promises and plans is essential for salvation and meaningful life (Hebrews 11:6).
3. *Relationship with God.* Building a personal relationship with God is central in the Bible. Knowing, worshiping, and serving God is considered a primary focus of life (John 17:3).
4. *Compassion and mercy.* The Bible teaches the importance of showing compassion and mercy to others, especially the poor, oppressed, and marginalized. The act of helping those in need is seen as an expression of one's faith (Micah 6:8; James 1:27).

5. *Justice and righteousness.* Pursuing justice and living righteously are values promoted in the Bible. God calls for fair treatment, ethical conduct, and standing up for what is just (Isaiah 1:17; Proverbs 21:3).
6. *Humility.* Humility is a highly regarded virtue in the Bible. Being humble and having a servant's heart is emphasized as an important aspect of the Christian life (Philippians 2:3–4; Matthew 23:12).
7. *Forgiveness.* Forgiveness is a significant theme in the Bible. Believers are called to forgive others as they have been forgiven by God. Forgiveness is essential for maintaining healthy relationships (Ephesians 4:32; Matthew 6:14–15).
8. *Hope.* The Bible offers the hope of eternal life and the promise of God's presence. This hope provides encouragement and perspective, reminding believers of the ultimate purpose of their lives (Romans 15:13; 1 Peter 1:3–4).
9. *Service.* Serving others and meeting their needs is a central aspect of Christian living. The Bible teaches that serving others is a way to serve God and express love (Matthew 25:35–40).
10. *Fruit of the Spirit.* The Bible lists the "Fruit of the Spirit" in Galatians 5:22–23, which includes love, joy, peace, patience, kindness, goodness, faithfulness, gentleness, and self-control. These qualities are seen as evidence of a life lived in accordance with God's will.
11. *Eternal perspective.* The Bible encourages believers to focus on eternal values rather than temporary worldly ones. This includes storing treasures in heaven and seeking the approval of God (Matthew 6:19–20; 2 Corinthians 4:18).

The Most Important Thing in Life

According to the Bible, what truly matters in life involves love, faith, relationships, compassion, justice, humility, forgiveness, hope, service, and eternal values. These principles guide us in our journey with God and in our relationships with others, making our lives meaningful and purposeful.

Now let's think about what's most important to you. Is it money? While money is useful, it doesn't guarantee happiness. Many wealthy people are unhappy.

Is it love? Love is crucial, but there's something even more essential. Without it, love won't thrive.

Is it happiness? Absolutely, happiness matters, but without what I'm about to tell you, it's hard to find.

The most crucial thing you'll ever have is good values—the Word of God. Values are what we consider most important, even above money, love, and happiness.

Values are what we believe in more than our feelings. In our modern time, feelings often seem more important, but that's not true.

Here's an example: Imagine craving junk food. You want it, but your value for staying healthy stops you. Values often clash with our feelings.

There's a necessary battle inside us: between what we feel and what we value. It's crucial not only for our own choices but also for how we treat others.

Consider this scenario: Your dog and a stranger are both drowning. Your instinct might be to save your pet first. But if you value human life more, it conflicts with your feelings for your dog.

Another situation: You're tempted to cheat on a test. You feel like it, but if you value honesty, you'll resist. It's that struggle between feelings and values.

Many wrongs in the world happen because people prioritize their feelings over higher moral values, like the Word of God. Murder, theft, and more arise from this conflict.

Good values—the Word of God—are incredibly important. Without them, the world would be a harsh place.

Remember, the best people, the kindest and most honest, battle their feelings daily. So should we all.

Understanding Who I Am in Christ!

Understanding who you are in Christ is crucial for several reasons:

1. *Identity and self-worth.* Knowing who you are in Christ helps establish a secure identity and self-worth. It teaches that your value isn't based on external factors or achievements but on being a beloved child of God.
2. *Purpose and calling.* Understanding your identity in Christ helps discern your purpose and calling in life. It aligns your life choices with God's plan and helps you use your gifts and talents for His glory.
3. *Freedom from condemnation.* It brings freedom from guilt, shame, and condemnation. Recognizing your forgiveness and righteousness in Christ allows you to live without the burden of past mistakes or insecurities.
4. *Strength and confidence.* Knowing who you are in Christ provides strength and confidence in facing life's challenges. It assures you of God's presence, guidance, and empowerment in every situation.
5. *Transformation and growth.* It promotes spiritual growth and transformation. Understanding your identity in Christ allows you to grow in faith, character, and maturity, becoming more Christlike.
6. *Healthy relationships.* It influences how you relate to others. When you understand your identity in Christ, you can

relate to others with love, grace, and compassion, fostering healthy relationships.

7. *Purposeful living.* It leads to a life lived with purpose and meaning. Understanding your identity helps you live a life aligned with God's will, making choices that honor Him.
8. *Hope and assurance.* It provides hope and assurance for the future. Knowing your identity in Christ assures you of God's promises and the hope of eternity spent with Him.

Understanding who you are in Christ shapes your perspective, choices, and relationships, enabling you to live a purposeful, confident, and fulfilled life rooted in God's love and grace.

Two of the most important questions in life are: Who is God, and who am I? These questions are linked because the God who created you has a purpose for your life. Life equals God plus You. Deep within your heart, there's a hope for greatness, a sense of eternity, and a desire for love, true peace, joy, and happiness. These desires come from your Creator. You might feel that there's more to life than your current situation.

Do you ever ask, "Who am I?"

The world teaches that people figure out who they are by being part of groups. These groups can be about things like race, where you come from, being a man or a woman, and how much money you have. Learning and adopting the values and behaviors of your society shape who you are. It's like society is molding you into being a part of it.

Important things like family, school, religion, and money really affect how people behave. These things help mold how a person acts and understands their role in the bigger picture of society.

In society, there are structures, like rules and roles, that guide how people interact. These interactions and relationships with others help create and show who you are.

Your sense of self, or who you think you are, comes from how you interact with others and the meanings you share with them. Building relationships with others and being a part of social activities are ways people create and confirm who they are.

Symbols and words also play a big part in making up who you are. They help express values and show which groups you belong to. The way people communicate with symbols and words is how they negotiate who they are.

In a nutshell, the world teaches us that our identity is shaped by being part of groups, learning from our surroundings, and interacting with others, all influenced by symbols and language.

"Who am I?" is a question we often ask subconsciously. It's even more challenging when the world tells you that who you are is found in your accomplishments, popularity, looks, or other superficial things. But when all that is peeled away, when I am sitting alone, who am I, really?

But the Bible teaches us in Romans 2 KJV: "And be not conformed to this world: but be ye transformed by the renewing of your mind, that ye may prove what is that good, and acceptable, and perfect, will of God."

So the Bible instructs us exactly how to be saved. Once we are born again into God's family (John 3:16–20), we find the true answer to our identity in Christ. In Christ, I am accepted, I am secured, and I am significant.

God defines my true identity

People in the Bible struggled with this concept as well. Moses asked God, "Who am I?" when commissioned by Him for a great purpose. "But Moses said to God, 'Who am I that I should go to Pharaoh and bring the children of Israel out of Egypt'" (Exodus 3:11)? God affirms who Moses is by stating His own name. He reassures Moses that He is with him, giving Moses a new identity, a new purpose, and new confidence. "God said to Moses, 'I AM WHO I AM.' And he said, 'Say this to the people of Israel: 'I AM has sent me to you" (Exodus 3:14).

In the same way, if I am insecure or unsure of who I am based on the world's standards, there is no need to fear.

Romans 8:37–39 states, "No, in all these things we are more than conquerors through him who loved us. For I am sure that neither death nor life, nor angels nor rulers, nor things present nor things to come, nor powers, nor height nor depth, nor anything else in all creation, will be able to separate us from the love of God in Christ Jesus our Lord."

I am not the Great "I Am," as declared in Exodus 3:14, where God identifies Himself to Moses. Instead, by the grace of God, I am what I am (1 Corinthians 15:10).

In Christ, I am accepted, I am secured, and I am significant.

In Christ, I have found my true identity:

- *A new creation.* If I'm in Christ, I am a new creation; the old is gone, and everything is new (2 Corinthians 5:17).
- *A child of God.* Through belief in His name, I am given the right to become God's child (John 1:12).
- *Alive in Christ.* Even when I was dead in my sins, God made me alive with Christ through His grace (Ephesians 2:5).
- *His workmanship.* I am His workmanship, created for good works in Christ (Ephesians 2:10).
- *Chosen by God.* I am part of a chosen race, a royal priesthood, a holy nation belonging to God (1 Peter 2:9).
- *Free.* The law of the Spirit of life in Christ has set me free from the law of sin and death (Romans 8:2).
- *Holy before Him.* He chose us to be holy and blameless in His sight (Ephesians 1:4).
- *Not condemned.* In Christ, there is no condemnation (Romans 8:1).
- *Mind of Christ.* I have the mind of Christ (1 Corinthians 2:16).
- *An overcomer.* I have overcome because the One in me is greater than the one in the world (1 John 4:4).
- *Spirit of wisdom and revelation.* I have the Spirit of wisdom and revelation in the knowledge of Him (Ephesians 1:17–18).
- *Righteousness of God.* In Christ, I have become the righteousness of God (2 Corinthians 5:21).

- *Established in righteousness.* I am established in righteousness and far from oppression (Isaiah 54:14).
- *Christ's authority.* I have been given authority to overcome all the power of the enemy (Luke 10:17–19).
- *Seated with Christ.* I am seated with Christ in the heavenly places (Ephesians 2:6).
- *Loved.* God so loved the world that He gave His Son for me (John 3:16).
- *Christ living in me.* I have been crucified with Christ, and Christ lives in me (Galatians 2:20).
- *God's peace.* The peace of God, beyond understanding, guards my heart and mind in Christ (Philippians 4:7).
- *Jesus's friend.* I am Jesus's friend, and He has made known everything He heard from the Father (John 15:15).
- *Temple of the Holy Spirit.* My body is the temple of the Holy Spirit (1 Corinthians 6:19).
- *Received abundant grace.* I have received the abundance of grace and the gift of righteousness (Romans 5:17).
- *Power of the Holy Spirit.* I will receive power when the Holy Spirit comes upon me (Acts 1:8).
- *Equipped for spiritual warfare.* I am equipped with the armor of God to stand against the enemy (Ephesians 6:10–18).
- *Redeemed.* I have redemption through Christ's blood, the forgiveness of sins (Ephesians 1:7).
- *Spirit of power, love, and self-control.* God has given me a spirit of power, love, and self-control (2 Timothy 1:7).
- *Christ's strength.* I am strengthened with all power according to His glorious might (Colossians 1:11).
- *Citizen of heaven.* My citizenship is in heaven, and I wait for the Lord Jesus Christ (Philippians 3:20).
- *Part of the body of Christ.* I am part of the body of Christ, with individual gifts (1 Corinthians 12:27).
- *Blessed with every spiritual blessing.* God has blessed me with every spiritual blessing in Christ (Ephesians 1:3).
- *Born again.* I have been born again through the eternal word of God (1 Peter 1:23).

- *Conqueror.* In all things, I am more than a conqueror through Him who loved me (Romans 8:37).
- *Strengthened with all power.* I am strengthened with all power for endurance and perseverance (Colossians 1:11).
- *A child of the light.* I am a child of light and not of darkness (1 Thessalonians 5:5).
- *Ambassador for Christ.* I am an ambassador for Christ, urging reconciliation with God (2 Corinthians 5:20).
- *Dead to sin and alive to God.* I consider myself dead to sin but alive to God in Christ Jesus (Romans 6:11).
- *Joint heir with Christ.* If I suffer with Him, I will be glorified with Him as a joint heir (Romans 8:17).
- *Salt of the earth.* I am the salt of the earth, bringing flavor to the world (Matthew 5:13).
- *Forgiven.* In Christ, I have redemption, the forgiveness of sins (Colossians 1:14).
- *God's gift of salvation.* I have been saved by grace through faith; it is God's gift (Ephesians 2:8).
- *Abundant life.* Christ came for me to have life and have it abundantly (John 10:10).
- *God's promises.* In Christ, all of God's promises find their "Yes" (2 Corinthians 1:20).
- *Home in heaven.* Jesus has prepared a place for me in His Father's house (John 14:1–3).

These affirmations define my identity, purpose, and position in Christ, affirming the profound love and grace God has lavished upon me.

Understanding How to Receive God's Blessings!

Understanding how to receive God's blessings is important for several reasons:

1. *Awareness of God's provision.* Understanding how to receive God's blessings helps us recognize that God is a provider. It allows you to acknowledge that every good thing comes from Him.
2. *Alignment with God's will.* Learning to receive God's blessings involves aligning with His will and purposes. It helps in discerning what God desires for your life and how to walk in obedience to Him.
3. *Gratitude and thankfulness.* Knowing how to receive God's blessings brings up an attitude of gratitude. It encourages acknowledging and appreciating God's goodness in your life.
4. *Increased faith.* Understanding the process of receiving God's blessings deepens your faith. It teaches reliance on God's promises and helps build trust in His provision.
5. *Stewardship.* It promotes responsible stewardship. Recognizing God's blessings encourages using them wisely and for His glory rather than selfish gain.
6. *Spiritual growth.* Learning to receive God's blessings involves spiritual maturity. It teaches patience, persever-

ance, and humility in waiting on God's timing and understanding His ways.

7. *Sharing and generosity*. Understanding God's blessings leads to a desire to share and bless others. It inspires a generous heart, following God's example of giving.
8. *Personal transformation*. It can lead to personal transformation. Embracing God's blessings can bring about positive changes in attitude, character, and outlook on life.
9. *Fosters relationship with God*. Knowing how to receive God's blessings strengthens your relationship with Him. It deepens intimacy with God as you recognize and respond to His blessings with faith and gratitude.
10. *Fulfillment and joy*. Embracing God's blessings brings fulfillment and joy. It brings a sense of contentment and satisfaction that comes from knowing you are in alignment with God's will and receiving His provision.

Understanding how to receive God's blessings involves acknowledging His sovereignty, aligning with His principles, and being open to His work in your life. It brings spiritual growth, gratitude, and a deeper relationship with Him.

Opening your heart to divine blessings. Receiving God's blessings is a fundamental desire for many people of faith. While blessings can come in various forms, the Bible provides guidance on how to position yourself to receive God's blessings. Here are some key principles to help you understand how to receive God's blessings:

1. *Seek a relationship with God*. A close and personal relationship with God is the foundation for receiving His blessings. Seek to know Him, love Him, and serve Him with your whole heart (Deuteronomy 4:29).
2. *Obey God's commands*. Obedience to God's commands is often linked to His blessings. In the Bible, God promises blessings to those who walk in His ways and keep His commandments (Deuteronomy 28:1–14).

3. *Trust in God's providence.* Trust that God knows what is best for you. Even in difficult circumstances, believe that God is in control and has a plan (Proverbs 3:5–6).
4. *Prayer and thanksgiving.* Prayer is a means of communication with God. Make your requests known to Him with thanksgiving (Philippians 4:6). Thank Him for His blessings, both seen and unseen.
5. *Generosity and giving.* The Bible encourages generosity and giving. When you give to others and to God's work, it can open the door for God to bless you in return (Malachi 3:10; Luke 6:38).
6. *Repentance and forgiveness.* When you confess your sins and seek God's forgiveness, it paves the way for blessings. Repentance is a turning away from sin and toward God (Acts 3:19).
7. *Seek God's kingdom.* Jesus taught that seeking God's kingdom and His righteousness should be a priority. When you prioritize God's will and purposes, you can trust that He will provide what you need (Matthew 6:33).
8. *Patience and faith.* Sometimes, God's blessings may not come immediately. Exercise patience and faith, trusting that God's timing is perfect (Hebrews 11:6).
9. *Contentment.* Learning to be content with what you have is a valuable principle. It doesn't mean you shouldn't seek blessings, but contentment allows you to appreciate and be thankful for what you currently have (1 Timothy 6:6–8).
10. *Community and fellowship.* Being part of a community of believers and experiencing fellowship with others can be a source of blessing and support (Hebrews 10:24–25).
11. *Serving others.* Blessings can also come through serving and helping others. Jesus emphasized the importance of serving and loving your neighbor (Mark 10:45).
12. *Remember God's promises.* The Bible is full of promises of God's blessings. Meditate on these promises and trust that God is faithful to fulfill them (2 Corinthians 1:20).

It's important to note that God's blessings may not always take the form of material wealth or success. They can also include spiritual growth, peace, wisdom, and a deeper relationship with God. Ultimately, receiving God's blessings involves a posture of faith, obedience, and trust in God's goodness and providence.

Dear family and friends, if you really want to know how to receive God's blessings and actually benefit from them, you must avail yourself of the opportunity to know the whys and hows of God's blessings.

The blessings of God are necessities for man. Without it, we can hardly survive.

After God created Adam and Eve, He blessed them and said, be fruitful and multiply.

That was the first blessing that was pronounced on man, and from that moment, man began to populate the earth.

The blessings of God become more necessary *after the fall of Adam* in the garden of Eden because *God cursed the earth,* and man must toil before he can get anything from the ground.

It is those who are blessed by God that can escape this curse. For them, they will labor a little and reap much because the blessings of God have canceled the established curse for their sake.

You must know how to receive God's blessings when you need them but much more, what to do to receive them. It is good for you to know how to receive God's blessings, but the truth is that God is willing and ready to bless whoever comes to Him.

A leper came to Jesus and said if you are willing, you can heal me. Jesus said I am willing, and He touched him (Mark 1:40–45). The man received his healing instantly.

It is the will of God for everyone to be blessed. That is why He wanted Jesus to die for everyone so that we can all receive the blessing of salvation.

Once you can follow His rules, you are qualified to receive the best from Him. That is how to receive God's blessings.

You Have to Make Your Choice!

God will not force His blessings on you, even though He wants you to be blessed.

You have to show Him that you want it. You have to ask for it. You must make your choice.

The children of Israel who were descendants of Abraham, the friend of God, by virtue of their birth, are qualified for God's blessings, *but God told them they have to earn it by obeying Him like their father Abraham did.*

In Deuteronomy 30:19, God put two options before them: life and death, blessings and cursing, and told them to choose the one they wanted.

The choice is yours, too, whether you want to be blessed by God or not. You have the power to choose.

God's Blessings Are Conditional

The blessings of God are based on certain conditions, mainly that of obeying God.

Whoever wants to be blessed must first understand the conditions, laws, rules, etc., attached to such blessings and abide by them.

Usually, that is how to receive God's blessings, as you will find in the Bible.

God told the children of Israel in Deuteronomy 28:1–13 that if they hearken to His words and obey His commandments, He will set them high above all nations.

He will make them the head and not the tail (Deuteronomy 28:13).

Should they fail to obey Him, He told them that curses would be the result.

> I call heaven and earth to record this day against you, that I have set before you life and death, blessing and cursing: therefore choose life, that both thou and thy seed may live: That

> thou mayest love the LORD thy God, and that thou mayest obey his voice, and that thou mayest cleave unto him. (Deuteronomy 30:19–20)

That is also the instruction of God for everyone who wants to receive good things from God. The Bible says we cannot remain in sin and pray that grace should abound (Romans 6:1).

How to Receive God's Blessings A Simple Guide

Dear loved ones,

Do you want to receive God's blessings and truly benefit from them? God's blessings are crucial for us; without them, life is tough. Let's understand how to get these blessings.

When God created Adam and Eve, He blessed them, asking them to multiply. This was the first blessing, and people began to fill the earth.

After Adam and Eve's mistake, God cursed the earth, making it hard for people to grow food. But those blessed by God escape this curse. They work less and gain more because God's blessings cancel out the curse.

Knowing how to get God's blessings is essential. God is always willing to bless those who come to Him. Just like a leper who asked Jesus to heal him, God wants to bless us too.

But there are conditions for receiving God's blessings. You must understand and obey God's rules. If you follow His guidance, He will bless you immensely.

Here's how:

1. *Give your life to God.* When you accept Jesus into your life, you're qualified for God's blessings.
2. *Obey God's commandments.* Living righteously pleases God, inviting His blessings.
3. *Ask God for blessings.* Pray and seek God's blessings.

4. *Be a blessing to others.* Help others; sometimes, blessings come through people.
5. *Trust God's plan.* Surrender to God's will and trust His timing.
6. *Prioritize God in your life.* Love God above everything else.
7. *Use your gifts and talents.* They can connect you to God's blessings.
8. *Make changes when needed.* Sometimes, changing your location or job is necessary.
9. *Tithe and give to God.* Giving to God's work attracts His blessings.
10. *Remember the poor.* Being kind to the less fortunate invites blessings.
11. *Be diligent and hardworking.* God blesses hard work.
12. *Be persistent in prayer.* Don't give up easily; persistence is key.

Remember, sometimes God doesn't grant blessings for a few reasons:

1. Not asking God for blessings.
2. Lacking faith in God's ability.
3. Having wrong motives for wanting blessings.
4. Not confessing and repenting of sins.
5. Not aligning with God's timing.
6. Lack of persistence in prayer.
7. Praying for things outside God's will.
8. Holding onto unforgiveness toward others.

God loves us and wants to bless us abundantly. By following these steps and avoiding hindrances, you can open the door to God's blessings in your life. Be blessed!

I do not expect you to be chasing after God's blessings, but on the contrary, the Bible says they will follow you once you are doing what is right.

> That is how to receive God's blessings.
> How amazing is our God, and how good is He to us!
> There is so much in His Word for us, and so much He wants to give us.
> We are truly blessed!

Understanding Your Ultimate Purpose

Understanding your ultimate purpose according to the Bible is crucial for several reasons:

1. *Clarity in life.* Knowing your ultimate purpose provides clarity and direction in life. It helps you focus on what truly matters and guides your decisions and actions.
2. *Alignment with God's will.* Understanding your ultimate purpose aligns you with God's will. It helps you discern what God desires for your life and how you can live in harmony with His plans.
3. *Fulfillment.* Discovering your ultimate purpose brings a sense of fulfillment and satisfaction. It allows you to live a meaningful and purpose-driven life, finding satisfaction in contributing to God's kingdom work.
4. *Identity.* Knowing your ultimate purpose helps you understand your identity in Christ. It provides a sense of belonging and significance, recognizing that you are part of God's divine plan.
5. *Guidance in decision-making.* Understanding your ultimate purpose serves as a compass in decision-making. It helps you make choices that are in line with God's intentions for your life.
6. *Impact and influence.* Discovering your ultimate purpose empowers you to make a positive impact on others. It

enables you to use your talents, gifts, and resources to bless and influence those around you.

7. *Eternal perspective.* Recognizing your ultimate purpose gives an eternal perspective. It shifts the focus from temporary pursuits to eternal values, emphasizing God's kingdom and His purposes.
8. *Resilience in trials.* Understanding your ultimate purpose provides strength and resilience during difficult times. It gives meaning to challenges, knowing that God is working through them to fulfill His purposes in your life.
9. *Service and stewardship.* Knowing your ultimate purpose encourages serving God and others. It promotes responsible stewardship of the gifts and opportunities entrusted to you.
10. *Relationship with God.* Understanding your ultimate purpose deepens your relationship with God. It allows you to seek Him for guidance, strength, and wisdom as you live out His intended purpose for your life.

Ultimately, understanding your ultimate purpose, according to the Bible, helps you live a life that honors God, brings fulfillment, and positively impacts the world around you.

According to the Bible, your ultimate purpose is to know, love, and serve God. This purpose is rooted in a relationship with God and is central to the Christian faith. Here are key aspects of your ultimate purpose according to the Bible:

1. *Know God.* Your primary purpose is to know God personally. This involves understanding who He is, His character, His attributes, and His ways. Jesus emphasized this in John 17:3, saying, "And this is eternal life, that they know you, the only true God, and Jesus Christ whom you have sent."
2. *Love God.* Loving God with all your heart, soul, and mind is one of the greatest commandments in the Bible (Matthew 22:37–38). Your purpose includes cultivating a deep and abiding love for God.

3. *Serve God.* Your purpose also involves serving God. This service can take many forms, such as using your gifts and talents for His glory, helping others, and spreading His love and message to the world (Romans 12:1).
4. *Follow God's will.* Understanding and following God's will for your life is an essential aspect of your purpose. This includes seeking His guidance and making choices that align with His moral and ethical principles (Proverbs 3:5–6).
5. *Fulfill the great commission.* Jesus instructed His followers to make disciples of all nations and teach them about Him (Matthew 28:19–20). Your purpose includes sharing the message of salvation and helping others come to faith in Christ.
6. *Reflect God's image.* You are created in the image of God (Genesis 1:27). Your purpose is to reflect His image by living in ways that reflect His love, compassion, and holiness.
7. *Seek holiness.* Pursuing holiness and righteous living is part of your purpose. God calls you to be holy as He is holy (1 Peter 1:16).
8. *Glorify God.* Your ultimate purpose is to glorify God in all that you do. Whether through your actions, words, or attitude, you are to bring glory to God (1 Corinthians 10:31).
9. *Find fulfillment and meaning.* True fulfillment and meaning in life are found in your relationship with God and living out your purpose in Him. When you fulfill your ultimate purpose, you experience a sense of significance and contentment.
10. *Eternal life.* Your ultimate purpose extends to the hope of eternal life with God. The Bible promises that those who believe in Jesus Christ will have eternal life in His presence (John 3:16).

Your ultimate purpose, according to the Bible, involves being closely connected to God. This journey looks different for everyone but revolves around growing in faith and living it out, guided by your relationship with God and His teachings.

Jesus prayed for everyone who would believe in Him through the teachings of others. He prayed that all believers would be united with God just as Jesus is united with the Father so the world would believe in God's message (John 17:20–21).

In Christ, through His sacrifice, we are forgiven and set free, chosen by God even before the world began to be holy and blameless in His sight (Ephesians 1:7–9, 1:3–4).

God's immense love and mercy gave us new life through Christ, showcasing His incredible grace (Ephesians 2:4–7).

Everything good comes from God, our unchanging Father (James 1:17).

We love God because He first loved us (1 John 4:19), and when we love Jesus and follow His teachings, God and Jesus make their home within us (John 14:23).

God's gift of His Son assures us that He'll freely give us everything we need (Romans 8:32).

Being "born again" is a spiritual experience Jesus talked about, connecting us to the kingdom of God (John 3:3, 3:6–8).

At your core, you're made up of spirit, soul, and body, with your spirit linking you to God and being the source of light and life (1 Thessalonians 5:23).

Jesus, referred to as the "Word of God," embodies the Father's communication and reveals God's nature (John 1:1–4).

God's Word, both through Jesus and the Bible, imparts His will and ways when received in the heart (1 Peter 1:23).

Through Jesus's teachings, we find the plan for our happiness and salvation, received through faith and grace (Ephesians 2:8–9).

Accepting God's grace means receiving Jesus and the Holy Spirit, marking us as God's possession (Ephesians 1:13–14).

God's words carry His Spirit and create life; they are spiritual and eternal (John 6:63; 2 Corinthians 4:18).

Revelation of Jesus comes through the Holy Spirit, often through the Scriptures, helping us grow spiritually (1 Peter 2:2–3).

Jesus is intimately connected to us, promising never to leave or reject us; He is our constant guide and mentor (Hebrews 13:5; Romans 8:29).

The Spirit reveals truth and glorifies Jesus, guiding us into unity with the Father and into holiness (John 16:13–14).

God desires a close, loving relationship with you. He made you to be connected to Him through Jesus. Jesus is the way to God, and being one with Him fulfills your purpose. This unity with Jesus was planned by God even before the world began.

God's aim is for you to be as close to Him as Jesus is, like family. Jesus has always been connected to God, even before everything existed.

From God's view, through Jesus, you're already perfect because of what Jesus did. Our journey involves understanding and agreeing with how God sees us.

Jesus leads us in this journey toward unity with God. He's both the path and the destination for us to be united with God. In this union with Jesus, we find completion and authority.

God created and designed you because it pleased Him. He's eager to shower you with kindness, favor, and acceptance, which is grace. God wants to be your loving Father, and just like a child depends on a parent, we rely on God's grace.

Our relationship with God starts with receiving from Him since He gave us life. We have nothing to give to God that we didn't receive from Him first.

As we receive God's goodness and grace, we experience His love. This understanding of God's goodness leads us to love and trust Him more and more. Loving God wholeheartedly is crucial, and it begins with God loving us first.

When we love Jesus and keep His teachings close, God and Jesus make their home within us. Loving Jesus means valuing His words, which are vital in this relationship.

Experiencing God's love is personal and heartfelt. If you want to know if God loves you, ask Him quietly in your heart. He'll show you how much He loves you, especially through Jesus's sacrifice on the cross.

God giving His Son for us demonstrates how much He's willing to freely give us everything we need.

Being "born again" is a spiritual change Jesus talked about, connecting us to God's kingdom.

At your core, you're spirit, soul, and body. Your spirit links you to God and guides your conscience. Your soul, which includes your mind and emotions, makes decisions based on information from your body and spirit.

Jesus Christ is called the "Word of God." He embodies everything about God. You can't separate God from His Word, which includes the Bible. Accepting God's Word means accepting Him.

When we believe and accept God's Word, we receive Jesus and His Spirit. This starts a new life that lasts forever, beginning with faith and grace, not because of anything we did ourselves.

God's words carry His Spirit and create life. Everything in God's kingdom is spiritual and eternal.

We understand more about Jesus and God through the Holy Spirit, often through the Bible. As we grow, His Word becomes a part of us.

Jesus is always with us, guiding us as our teacher, friend, protector, and more. He'll never leave or reject us. He helps us understand God and leads us closer to Him.

The Holy Spirit reveals truth within us, showing us God's messages and guiding us closer to Jesus and the Father.

To my dear family and friends, I've chosen to follow Jesus. I hope you can open your heart to look toward Him, trust Him, and find peace in Him. It's all about accepting the love and kindness that your Heavenly Father gives through Jesus Christ.

There's a song called "I Have Decided to Follow Jesus" by Leslie B. Tucker that really means a lot to me. Here, I quote it for you:

> I have decided to follow Jesus; I have decided to follow Jesus; I have decided to follow Jesus; No turning back, no turning back.
>
> Tho' none go with me, I still will follow, Tho' none go with me I still will follow, Tho'

none go with me, I still will follow; No turning back, no turning back.

My cross I'll carry, till I see Jesus; My cross I'll carry till I see Jesus, My cross I'll carry till I see Jesus; No turning back, No turning back.

The world behind me, the cross before me, The world behind me, the cross before me; The world behind me, the cross before me; No turning back, no turning back.

Will you decide now to follow Jesus? Will you decide now to follow Jesus? Will you decide now to follow Jesus? No turning back, no turning back.

Understanding God Wants You Come Home

Understanding that God wants you to come home is important for several reasons:

1. *Reconciliation.* God desires reconciliation with humanity. Recognizing that God wants you to come home means understanding His longing for a restored relationship with each individual.
2. *Unconditional love.* It reflects God's unconditional love. Knowing that God wants you to come home showcases His deep love and desire to embrace you regardless of past mistakes or circumstances.
3. *Forgiveness.* Understanding God's invitation to come home means acknowledging His willingness to forgive. It emphasizes God's grace and willingness to offer forgiveness and a fresh start.
4. *Restoration.* It signifies God's desire for restoration and wholeness. Coming home to God offers the opportunity to experience spiritual, emotional, and sometimes even physical restoration.
5. *Purpose and fulfillment.* Recognizing God's call to come home allows for the discovery of purpose and fulfillment. It aligns individuals with their intended relationship with God, leading to a life of meaning and satisfaction.

6. *Eternal life.* Accepting God's invitation to come home leads to the promise of eternal life. It assures believers of an eternal home in God's presence.
7. *Hope and comfort.* Understanding that God wants you to come home brings hope and comfort, especially in challenging times. It assures believers of God's constant presence and support.
8. *Salvation.* Coming home to God is the path to salvation. It leads to a transformed life and a secure future in God's kingdom.
9. *Receiving God's blessings.* Accepting God's invitation to come home opens the door to experiencing His blessings, guidance, and provision in life.
10. *Living in God's will.* Coming home to God means aligning with His will and purpose for your life. It signifies a commitment to live according to His teachings and follow His guidance.

Understanding that God wants you to come home is an invitation to experience His love, forgiveness, and presence, offering a path to a meaningful and eternal relationship with Him.

In the Bible, the idea of "coming home" can have various spiritual and symbolic meanings. Here are a few ways to understand what it means to come home according to the Bible:

1. *Repentance and return to God.* One of the significant themes of coming home in the Bible is the concept of repentance and returning to God. When individuals turn away from sin and disobedience and turn back to God, it is often described as coming home (Luke 15:7). The parable of the prodigal son in Luke 15:11–32 illustrates this beautifully, where the wayward son returns to his father's house, symbolizing repentance, and reconciliation with God.
2. *Salvation and finding rest.* Coming home can also represent finding salvation and rest in God. Jesus invites those who

are weary and burdened to come to Him for rest, symbolizing a spiritual homecoming (Matthew 11:28).

3. *Heavenly home.* The Bible speaks of believers having a heavenly home in God's presence. This is the ultimate homecoming, where believers will dwell with God for eternity. In John 14:2–3, Jesus speaks of preparing a place for His followers in His Father's house, which represents the heavenly homecoming.
4. *Finding belonging in the church.* The local church is often referred to as a spiritual family and home for believers. Coming home can mean finding a sense of belonging, fellowship, and community within a local congregation (Ephesians 2:19).
5. *Returning to God's ways.* Coming home can also signify returning to God's ways and living in accordance with His commandments. It represents aligning one's life with God's will and guidance (Isaiah 55:7).
6. *Restoration and renewal.* The process of coming home can involve restoration and renewal. It means experiencing God's grace and forgiveness, which bring about a sense of renewal and a fresh start (Joel 2:25).
7. *Reconciliation with others.* Coming home can also involve reconciliation and restored relationships with others. The Bible encourages believers to seek peace and reconciliation with fellow believers, representing a homecoming to unity and harmony (Matthew 5:23–24).
8. *Finding purpose and identity.* Sometimes, coming home can also relate to discovering one's true purpose and identity in God. It means understanding who you are in Christ and the unique role you play in God's kingdom (Ephesians 2:10).

In various biblical contexts, coming home signifies a return to God's presence, grace, and love, whether through repentance, salvation, reconciliation, or the ultimate hope of a heavenly home. It represents a spiritual journey of restoration, renewal, and finding one's true belonging and purpose in God's plan.

God Loves You
And He Wants You to Come Home
Finding Home with God

We all long for home deep within our hearts. Two thousand years ago, Jesus came to show us who God really is and to be the way back home to our Heavenly Father. Would you like to receive this precious gift?

In the Book of John, it tells us that before the world began, Jesus was there with God. He brought life and light to the world, but sadly, not everyone recognized Him. Yet, for those who did, they became God's own children, not because of any human effort but through God's love.

You can accept Jesus and become a child of God by simply saying yes to His invitation to come home. It's a free gift, and the price for your salvation has already been paid.

If you want to come home, here's a prayer that might help express your feelings to God. Remember, it's not the words that save you, but the openness of your heart toward your Heavenly Father:

> Heavenly Father, I want to come home. I believe you love me and sent Jesus to save me. I turn from my old ways and embrace Jesus. I received His life in exchange for my old life. I trust Jesus alone to rescue me. Thank you, Jesus, for forgiving me. I want to follow and serve you always. Thank you for being my way back home. Amen.

Your New Relationship with God

As you begin this new journey, knowing you're loved, you'll discover God as your Father. By believing in Jesus, you're assured of incredible truths found in the Bible. Here are a few that may encourage you:

- You are God's child (John 1:12–13).
- God loves you immensely (1 John 3:1).
- You have eternal life through Jesus (John 3:16).
- God placed His Spirit within you (2 Corinthians 1:21–22).
- You can talk directly to God (Matthew 7:7–11).
- Nothing can separate you from God's love (Romans 8:38–39).

Practical Steps on Your Journey

1. Get a Bible and read it every day. Start with the Gospel of John.
2. Cultivate your relationship with God by talking to Him regularly.
3. Connect with other believers in a church or gathering.
4. Share your decision with a close friend for support and encouragement.

To my dear family and friends

I've thought about many good things to say to all of you, like expressing pride in who you are, thanking you for bringing joy into my life, seeking forgiveness for any hurt I've caused, celebrating your achievements, and more. But what matters most to me is that each one of you experiences a spiritual rebirth and finds salvation.

The most vital thing to me is that you've embraced God's love, received eternal life, and welcomed the Holy Spirit into your hearts (John 3:16; Acts 1:8). I care deeply for all of you!

One song that's deeply touched me is "Amazing Grace [My Chains Are Gone]." It's a beautiful modern version of the classic hymn "Amazing Grace" penned by Chris Tomlin, Louie Giglio, and

John Newton. It's moved me profoundly, and I hope it touches your heart too!

> Amazing grace how sweet the sound
> That saved a wretch like me
> I once was lost, but now I'm found
> Was blind, but now I see
> My chains are gone
> I've been set free My God
> my Savior has ransomed me
> And like a flood, His mercy reigns
> Unending love, amazing grace
> The Lord has promised good to me
> His word my hope secures
> He will my shield and portion be
> As long as life endures
> My chains are gone
> I've been set free My God
> my Savior has ransomed me
> And like a flood, His mercy reigns
> Unending love, amazing grace
> The earth shall soon dissolve like snow
> The sun forbear to shine
> But God, who called me here below
> Will be forever mine
> Will be forever mine
> You are forever mine

Understanding Life Lessons from People in the Bible

Understanding life's lessons from the people in the Bible is crucial for several reasons:

1. *Wisdom and guidance.* The stories in the Bible often contain valuable lessons about human nature, morality, and decision-making. Learning from the successes and failures of biblical figures can provide us with guidance on how to navigate similar situations in our lives.
2. *Inspiration and encouragement.* Many biblical characters faced adversity, yet they found strength, faith, and resilience in challenging times. Their stories can inspire and encourage us to persevere through our own struggles.
3. *Moral and ethical values.* The Bible presents various moral and ethical dilemmas and how individuals deal with them. Understanding these stories helps shape our moral compass and ethical decision-making.
4. *Spiritual growth.* Exploring the lives of biblical figures deepens our spiritual understanding and fosters personal growth. It can lead to a deeper connection with God and a better understanding of our purpose in life.
5. *Context and perspective.* Studying biblical narratives provides historical and cultural context. It helps us appreciate the different contexts in which people lived and the principles they upheld, allowing for a broader perspective on life.

6. *Avoiding mistakes.* By learning from the mistakes of biblical characters, we can avoid repeating similar errors in our lives. Understanding their consequences can guide us toward making wiser choices.

Overall, understanding life's lessons from the people in the Bible can enrich our lives, help us make better decisions, and guide us on our spiritual journey.

Here is a simplified summary of valuable life lessons from various Bible figures that we can learn. Lessons that we can incorporate into our own lives.

1. *Adam and Eve.* Learn from mistakes and take responsibility for your actions.
2. *Cain and Abel.* Avoid jealousy and strive for positive relationships with others.
3. *Noah.* Follow divine guidance even when it seems unconventional; trust in God's promises.
4. *Lot.* Make wise choices and avoid compromising principles.
5. *Ishmael.* Embrace resilience in challenging circumstances.
6. *Abraham.* Demonstrate faith, even in uncertainty.
7. *Sarah.* Practice patience and trust in divine timing.
8. *Isaac.* Illustrate obedience, sacrifice, and continuity of faith.
9. *Hagar.* Exhibit strength in difficult situations.
10. *Rebekah.* Demonstrate discernment and trust in divine guidance.
11. *Esau.* Reflect on the consequences of impulsive decisions.
12. *Jacob.* Embrace growth, resilience, and reconciliation.
13. *Rachel.* Understand the complexities of love and relationships.
14. *Laban.* Recognize the consequences of deception and value integrity.
15. *Joseph.* Display resilience, forgiveness, and faith in divine providence.
16. *Reuben.* Consider the impact of impulsive decisions on relationships.

17. *Judah*. Emphasize growth, redemption, and taking responsibility.
18. *Moses*. Learn about leadership, obedience, and perseverance.
19. *Jethro*. Value wisdom and seek guidance from mentors.
20. *Aaron*. Emphasize collaboration and support in achieving shared goals.
21. *Nadab and Abihu*. Approach sacred matters with reverence and follow divine instructions.
22. *Miriam*. Recognize the impact of leadership and the strength of familial bonds.
23. *Caleb*. Exhibit faith, courage, and perseverance in challenging situations.
24. *Korah*. Avoid rebellion and respect divinely appointed authority.
25. *Eleazar*. Display loyalty, commitment, and courage in the face of adversity.
26. *Balaam*. Beware of compromising principles for personal gain.
27. *Joshua*. Embody leadership, faith, and the fulfillment of promises.
28. *Jephthah*. Reflect on the consequences of rash vows and commitments.
29. *Samson*. Understand the consequences of personal weaknesses and seek redemption.
30. *Delilah*. Be aware of the impact of betrayal and manipulation in relationships.
31. *Ruth*. Embrace loyalty, kindness, and the transformative power of love.
32. *Naomi*. Demonstrate resilience, even in the face of loss.
33. *Boaz*. Showcase generosity, integrity, and compassion.
34. *Hannah*. Illustrate faith, prayer, and the fulfillment of promises.
35. *Eli*. Recognize the consequences of neglecting responsibilities.
36. *Samuel*. Embrace humility, obedience, and dedication to divine guidance.

37. *Saul.* Be wary of the perils of disobedience and rejecting divine guidance.
38. *David.* Reflect on triumphs, challenges, and the enduring nature of God's mercy.
39. *Jonathan.* Emphasize loyalty, friendship, and sacrifice in relationships.
40. *Abigail.* Display wisdom, diplomacy, and the positive impact of peacemaking.
41. *Abner.* Understand the complexities of power, loyalty, and leadership.
42. *Joseph's mighty men.* Showcase valor, loyalty, and commitment to a common purpose.
43. *Bathsheba.* Learn from the consequences of choices, embrace redemption, and seek hope in challenging circumstances.
44. *Solomon.* Recognize the responsibilities and challenges of leadership.
45. *Jeroboam.* Understand the dangers of rebellion and the consequences of straying from divine guidance.
46. *Elijah.* Embody faith, boldness, and perseverance in adversity.
47. *Elisha.* Illustrate the transformative power of faith and dedication to serving God.
48. *Jehu.* Acknowledge the complexities of zeal, judgment, and carrying out divine directives.
49. *Hezekiah.* Learn from his commitment to reform, trust in God, and the miraculous deliverance of Jerusalem.
50. *Josiah.* Embrace righteous leadership, religious reform, and the pursuit of spiritual renewal.
51. *Rehoboam.* Be cautious of pride, harsh governance, and the consequences of poor leadership.
52. *Asa.* Demonstrate faithfulness, reliance on God, and the pursuit of spiritual integrity.
53. *Joash.* Understand the complexities of leadership, the influence of mentorship, and the challenges of maintaining faithfulness over time.

54. *Uzziah*. Beware of the perils of pride and the importance of acknowledging divine authority.
55. *Manasseh*. Learn from his journey of repentance and the possibility of finding redemption.
56. *Zerubbabel*. Showcase determination, perseverance, and commitment to fulfilling divine purposes.
57. *Ezra*. Emphasize the importance of spiritual renewal, adherence to divine guidance, and commitment to God's word.
58. *Nehemiah*. Illustrate leadership.

Certainly! Here's a condensed summary of life lessons from the remaining Bible figures:

59. *Mordecai and Esther*. Display bravery, strategic thinking, and the providence of God in challenging circumstances.
60. *Haman*. Understand the dangers of pride, hatred, and the consequences of seeking personal gain at others' expense.
61. *Job*. Learn from profound suffering, faith, and eventual restoration, showcasing endurance and trust in God.
62. *Isaiah*. Emphasize the themes of repentance, redemption, and the anticipation of a future Messiah.
63. *Jeremiah*. Highlight the challenges of delivering difficult truths, emphasizing faithfulness in fulfilling one's calling.
64. *Daniel*. Illustrate unwavering faith, wisdom, and resilience in the face of adversity, showcasing the triumph of devotion to God.
65. *Nebuchadnezzar*. Embrace humility and acknowledge God's sovereignty, recognizing the transformative impact of divine intervention.
66. *Joseph (coat of many colors)*. Exhibit resilience, forgiveness, and faith in divine providence amid trials.
67. *Joseph (Mary's husband)*. Demonstrate trust, acceptance, and commitment to God's plan even in uncertain circumstances.

68. *Herod the Great.* Understand the dangers of unchecked power, political intrigue, and cruelty.
69. *Matthew.* Learn about discipleship, dedication to sharing the Gospel, and the impact of encountering Jesus.
70. *Mary (mother of Jesus).* Exhibit faith, humility, and obedience, recognizing the privilege of being chosen for divine purposes.
71. *Peter.* Showcase loyalty, humility, and the transformative power of encountering Jesus.
72. *Judas Iscariot.* Reflect on the dangers of greed, betrayal, and the consequences of personal choices.
73. *Pilate.* Understand the complexities of balancing political considerations with ethical responsibilities.
74. *Zacharias.* Emphasize trust and faith in divine promises, overcoming doubt.
75. *Elizabeth.* Illustrate faithfulness, resilience, and the recognition of unexpected blessings.
76. *James.* Highlight familial ties, encounters with the risen Christ, and the transformative power of grace.
77. *Martha.* Balance serving with being present and understanding the various dimensions of discipleship.
78. *John the Baptist.* Embrace humility, dedication to preparing the way for God's kingdom, and recognizing the Messiah.
79. *Nicodemus.* Learn about the complexities of faith, encountering truth, and personal transformation.
80. *Caiaphas.* Reflect on the ethical challenges faced by leaders and the consequences of their decisions.
81. *John.* Understand themes of love, discipleship, and the mysteries of faith through the lens of a close relationship with Jesus.
82. *Mary Magdalene.* Embody loyalty, encountering Jesus, and the transformative power of grace and redemption.
83. *Thomas.* Illustrate themes of belief, evidence, and the transformative power of encountering truth.
84. *Stephen.* Showcase boldness, steadfast faith, and the challenges faced by early Christian martyrs.

85. *Philip*. Emphasize openness to divine guidance, inclusivity in sharing the Gospel, and the strength found in Christian camaraderie.
86. *Paul*. Illustrate the power of grace, redemption, and the impact of a life surrendered to Christ.
87. *Cornelius*. Display the inclusivity of God's grace and the breaking down of cultural barriers in the early church.
88. *Herod Agrippa I*. Understand the challenges faced by the early Christian community in the context of political and religious dynamics.
89. *John Mark*. Emphasize growth, resilience, and the impact of personal setbacks on the journey of faith.
90. *Barnabas*. Showcase encouragement, support, mentorship, and the positive impact of nurturing others in their faith.
91. *Silas*. Highlight the strength found in Christian camaraderie, facing challenges and triumphs in early Christian mission work.
92. *Luke*. Appreciate the detailed and compassionate portrayal of Jesus's life, ministry, and the early Christian community in his writings.
93. *Aquila and Priscilla*. Illustrate the collaborative nature of Christian service, the importance of mentorship, and the positive impact of nurturing others in their faith.
94. *Timothy*. Emphasize commitment to the Gospel, mentorship, and the challenges faced by early Christian leaders.
95. *James (brother of Jesus)*. Embody themes of family ties, encounters with the risen Christ, and the transformative power of grace.
96. *Martha (sister of Lazarus)*. Understand the various dimensions of discipleship, balancing action with contemplation.
97. *John Mark*. Learn from the journey of growth, resilience, and restoration after setbacks.
98. *Barnabas*. Emphasize encouragement, support, mentorship, and the positive impact of nurturing others in their faith.

99. *Silas.* Highlight the strength found in Christian camaraderie, facing challenges and triumphs in early Christian mission work

Absolutely, here's a concise summary of life lessons from the remaining Bible figures:

100. *Luke.* Appreciate the detailed and compassionate portrayal of Jesus's life, ministry, and the early Christian community in his writings.
101. *Aquila and Priscilla.* Illustrate the collaborative nature of Christian service, the importance of mentorship, and the positive impact of nurturing others in their faith.
102. *Timothy.* Emphasize commitment to the Gospel, mentorship, and the challenges faced by early Christian leaders.
103. *James (brother of Jesus).* Embody themes of family ties, encounters with the risen Christ, and the transformative power of grace.
104. *Martha (sister of Lazarus).* Understand the various dimensions of discipleship, balancing action with contemplation.
105. *John Mark.* Learn from the journey of growth, resilience, and restoration after setbacks.
106. *Barnabas.* Emphasize encouragement, support, mentorship, and the positive impact of nurturing others in their faith.
107. *Silas.* Highlight the strength found in Christian camaraderie, facing challenges and triumphs in early Christian mission work.
108. *Luke.* Appreciate the detailed and compassionate portrayal of Jesus's life, ministry, and the early Christian community in his writings.
109. *Aquila and Priscilla.* Illustrate the collaborative nature of Christian service, the importance of mentorship, and the positive impact of nurturing others in their faith.
110. *Timothy.* Emphasize commitment to the Gospel, mentorship, and the challenges faced by early Christian leaders.

111. *James (brother of Jesus).* Embody themes of family ties, encounters with the risen Christ, and the transformative power of grace.
112. *Martha (sister of Lazarus).* Understand the various dimensions of discipleship, balancing action with contemplation.
113. *John Mark.* Learn from the journey of growth, resilience, and restoration after setbacks.
114. *Barnabas.* Emphasize encouragement, support, mentorship, and the positive impact of nurturing others in their faith.
115. *Silas.* Highlight the strength found in Christian camaraderie, facing challenges and triumphs in early Christian mission work.
116. *Paul.* Showcase the power of grace, redemption, and the impact of a life surrendered to Christ.
117. *Cornelius.* Display the inclusivity of God's grace and the breaking down cultural barriers in the early church.
118. *Herod Agrippa I.* Understand the challenges faced by the early Christian community in the context of political and religious dynamics.
119. *John Mark.* Emphasize growth, resilience, and the impact of personal setbacks on the journey of faith.
120. *Barnabas.* Showcase encouragement, support, mentorship, and the positive impact of nurturing others in their faith.
121. *Silas.* Highlight the strength found in Christian camaraderie, facing challenges and triumphs in early Christian mission work.

Certainly, here's a concise summary of life lessons from the remaining Bible figures:

122. *Luke.* Appreciate the detailed and compassionate portrayal of Jesus's life, ministry, and the early Christian community in his writings.

123. *Aquila and Priscilla.* Illustrate the collaborative nature of Christian service, the importance of mentorship, and the positive impact of nurturing others in their faith.
124. *Timothy.* Emphasize commitment to the Gospel, mentorship, and the challenges faced by early Christian leaders.
125. *James (brother of Jesus).* Embody themes of family ties, encounters with the risen Christ, and the transformative power of grace.
126. *Martha (sister of Lazarus).* Understand the various dimensions of discipleship, balancing action with contemplation.
127. *John Mark.* Learn from the journey of growth, resilience, and restoration after setbacks.
128. *Barnabas.* Emphasize encouragement, support, mentorship, and the positive impact of nurturing others in their faith.
129. *Silas.* Highlight the strength found in Christian camaraderie, facing challenges and triumphs in early Christian mission work.
130. *Luke.* Appreciate the detailed and compassionate portrayal of Jesus's life, ministry, and the early Christian community in his writings.
131. *Aquila and Priscilla.* Illustrate the collaborative nature of Christian service, the importance of mentorship, and the positive impact of nurturing others in their faith.
132. *Timothy.* Emphasize commitment to the Gospel, mentorship, and the challenges faced by early Christian leaders.
133. *James (brother of Jesus).* Embody themes of family ties, encounters with the risen Christ, and the transformative power of grace.
134. *Martha (sister of Lazarus).* Understand the various dimensions of discipleship, balancing action with contemplation.
135. *John Mark.* Learn from the journey of growth, resilience, and restoration after setbacks.
136. *Barnabas.* Emphasize encouragement, support, mentorship, and the positive impact of nurturing others in their faith.

137. *Silas*. Highlight the strength found in Christian camaraderie, facing challenges and triumphs in early Christian mission work.
138. *Paul*. Showcase the power of grace, redemption, and the impact of a life surrendered to Christ.
139. *Cornelius*. Display the inclusivity of God's grace and the breaking down of cultural barriers in the early church.
140. *Herod Agrippa I*. Understand the challenges faced by the early Christian community in the context of political and religious dynamics.
141. *John Mark*. Emphasize growth, resilience, and the impact of personal setbacks on the journey of faith.
142. *Barnabas*. Showcase encouragement, support, mentorship, and the positive impact of nurturing others in their faith.
143. *Silas*. Highlight the strength found in Christian camaraderie, facing challenges and triumphs in early Christian mission work.

Family Prayers

Family prayers are essential for a few key reasons:

1. *Unity and connection.* When families pray together, it brings them closer, creating a stronger bond and a sense of togetherness.
2. *Growing together.* Praying as a family helps everyone grow spiritually, sharing in each other's faith journeys.
3. *Shared beliefs.* It reinforces the values and beliefs that hold the family together, making sure everyone is on the same page spiritually.
4. *Support in tough times.* Praying together offers support during hard times, giving family members a way to find comfort in their faith as a group.
5. *Teaching and learning.* It's a chance for parents to teach their kids about prayer and the importance of faith.
6. *Gratitude and sharing.* Family prayers help everyone appreciate what they have and share their feelings and needs openly.
7. *Solving problems.* It can also help solve arguments or issues by bringing everyone together to seek forgiveness and peace.
8. *Mental and emotional health.* Regular family prayers can bring peace of mind and comfort, helping everyone feel better mentally and emotionally.
9. *Establishing a habit.* It makes prayer a regular part of life, showing how important it is in good and tough times.

10. *Connecting with God.* Most importantly, family prayers help the family feel closer to God, giving them a way to ask for guidance and strength together.

Ultimately, family prayer brings the family closer together and closer to God. It strengthens their bond, helps them grow spiritually, and provides a supportive, comforting space where they can share their faith, values, needs, and gratitude as a unified unit.

So let us pray together

Heavenly Father, I thank you for the gift of my family. Thank You for the gift of being a parent and a grandparent.

Thank You for showing me an example of the love, grace, wisdom, and discipline of a parent. I'm so grateful that You have given us Your Word. It is a lamp for our feet and a light for the path in front of us.

Just like me, my adult children need wisdom in this stage of their lives. They need Your wisdom as they make decisions every day. Some decisions will have little impact on their lives, but others have the ability to change their lives and the lives of other people drastically, for the good or for the bad. My prayer is that You would guide them in making wise decisions. When they are faced with a challenging decision, I pray that they will seek You out in prayer.

May they root their life choices and values in the truth of Your good news. Remind them of the eternal value the choices they make today serve. And help them grow and mature even through poor decisions. In all things, may their life decisions lead them back to You.

Please protect my adult children and their family from anything that would cause them to suffer harm. I pray that they will find a hiding place in You. And that the world and its influences would not entice them. Please protect them not only physically but mentally, emotionally, and spiritually.

My prayer is that You will lead them in the way they should go. When they come to face a fork in the road, would You give them clarity and light up their path. Help them to seek You in the different areas of their lives and to desire Your will for them. When they are in doubt, I pray that You will surround them with those who are wise and will point them back to You.

Remind them to make You a part of their life decisions and to seek Your will for their lives. May they not only grow spiritually in their knowledge of You and their relationship with You, but I pray that through it, You would mold and shape them to look more like You. I pray that their character will be refined and that it will encourage further growth in their relationships, in their career, and in the way that they live their lives. May their changed hearts and lives be a picture of Your goodness and love.

Lord, thank you for the gift of my daughter-in-law and my sons-in-law(s)

They are such a light to my life. Thank you for the gift of family! May they continue to glorify You in all that they do. May You be at the forefront of their mind and the driving force for all their actions. Lord, what a privilege it is to see my grandchildren growing up and learning about You. Thank You, Father, for each little life, and I lift each one to You, Lord, and pray that by Your grace and love, You would surround them with Your love throughout their lives.

Guard and guide them all. I pray and uphold and protect them. May each one come to know You, Lord, as their personal Savior, and may they all come to a deep understanding of all You are and all that You have done for them. Oh Lord, I pray most earnestly that each one would accept You into their hearts and lives as their Lord and Savior.

I pray that as they grow into their teens and become young adults, You would keep their hearts and minds turned to You and trust in Jesus for their every need. Protect each one from the philosophies and mindset of the world that are so contrary to the truth of Scripture, and may each one grow in grace and become strong in their faith as they develop in wisdom and discernment.

Protect them from the evils of this age, keep them from temptations, and help them to live godly lives and develop as responsible adults who will teach their own children the wonderful truth of Salvation through Christ Jesus our Lord. In His name, I pray.

Grandpa's prayer for the future spouse of my grandchildren

Dear Heavenly Father, thank You for the lives of each of my lovely grandchildren that You have so graciously brought into my life. They all give me such joy and pleasure, for which I praise and thank You.

Lord, I pray as they grow up into adulthood, You will continue to lead and guide, to instruct, and to correct them. Father, I also pray that You would develop in each one a heavenly perspective and a true understanding of the Christian life and spiritual maturity so that they grow in grace and a right relationship with You.

Heavenly Father, I pray that you would bring the right spouse into the life of each of these dear grandchildren of mine, I pray. In Your grace, I pray that they be granted the husband or wife of Your choice so that together, they may become a threefold cord with You, which is not easily broken.

Thank You, Lord, so much for every one of my grandchildren. Into Your hands, I commit each one. May they discover Your calling on their lives so that they develop into mighty men and women who love You deeply and trust in You implicitly. In Jesus's name, I pray.

My prayers for my wife

Heavenly Father, thank You for my wife and all that she means to me. Thank You for bringing such a good woman into my life to be my helper, friend, and comfort. Thank You for her love for You, Lord, and I pray that day by day, our marriage may become stronger so that together we may grow in grace and that our mutual love for each other and for You may blossom into the marriage partnership that You desire for each of Your children. Bless our lives together and unite us in a closer bond of unity with each other so that together we may stand shoulder to shoulder as we carry out the lifework that You have given to us, to the glory of Your name.

Dear Lord, I pray that Your love will pour over my wife. Engrave in her heart and speak into her thoughts that You see her and hear the cries of her heart. Help her lean into the truth of who You say she is and find comfort in Your unfailing love. Thank You, Lord, for the gift of my dear wife. Lord, I know that a good and virtuous woman is worth more than rubies and precious stones. Help me to be the husband that You would have me be, to encourage her and love her as Christ loved the church, and to think of her needs and wishes before my own. Help me to cleave to my wife as You have instructed in Your Word, and may we grow ever closer to each other and to You as we daily spend time in fellowship with one another and in Your presence together. May she grow strong in the Lord and the power of Your might, and protect her mind and thoughts, I pray, from the influences of the world. Help her fix her heart and mind on the Lord Jesus, and may she continue to place her full trust and hope in You. Give her a gentle spirit and a tender heart, and may she become more and more a woman where her inner beauty shines out as the example of one who loves and fears the Lord. And help me to be a good and loving husband so that together we can witness Your authority in our lives and marriage. In Jesus's name, I pray.

Prayer for my friends

Heavenly Father, how gracious You are to bring into my life my many precious friends, all of whom have become so special to me in their own individual and unique ways.

I feel so blessed to be surrounded by so many dear people that I love and care for and for the knowledge that they also love and care for me too. Thank You for the support that I have so often received from different ones during those times of difficulty and pain.

Thank You also for the valuable lessons that I have learned. Even though some have been very difficult, I have been enabled, through the loving support and encouragement of my friends, to grow spiritually and emotionally and gain wisdom and insight in so many important ways.

Help me to be the sort of friend that is always there for others. An ear to listen, a hand to help, and a heart to comfort. And help me to grow in grace and in a knowledge of Jesus so that I may be His hands, His ears, His heart, and His comfort to the many precious people that You have placed in my life.

Dear Lord, again, thank You for my friends, neighbors, and known and unknown people in my circle. I pray that You would put Your hand on their lives. I pray that You would put inside their hearts a thirst to live by Your standards and to always seek Your love every single day of their lives. Lord, I thank You now for all the blessings that You will pour into their lives. In Jesus's name, I pray, amen.

Salvation Prayer for All

Dear Heavenly Father God, I pray for the salvation of men and women throughout our neighborhood, city, county, and the world who have not come to a saving faith in the Lord Jesus Christ. Lord, we know that it is not Your will that anyone should perish but that all should come to faith in the Lord Jesus as their Savior.

> The Lord is not slack concerning his promise, as some men count slackness; but is long-suffering to us-ward, not willing that any should perish, but that all should come to repentance. (2 Peter 3:9 KJV)

Father, I lift all people to You and pray that in Your long-suffering mercy, You would draw close to each and every one. I pray that the light of Your love would shine into their hearts and that the truth of Your Word would convict their inner soul of their need for a Savior.

Thank You for sending Christ Jesus into the world to be born and live among us. Thank You that He was willing to die on the cross for sinners, to give His life as a ransom for many, so as to provide salvation for all who would believe in Him as Savior.

> And we have seen and do testify that the Father sent the Son to be the Saviour of the world. (1 John 4:14 KJV)

He that dwelleth in the secret place of the most High shall abide under the shadow of the Almighty.

I will say of the LORD, He is my refuge and my fortress: my God; in him will I trust.

Surely he shall deliver thee from the snare of the fowler, and from the noisome pestilence.

He shall cover thee with his feathers, and under his wings shalt thou trust: his truth shall be thy shield and buckler.

Thou shalt not be afraid for the terror by night; nor for the arrow that flieth by day;

Nor for the pestilence that walketh in darkness; nor for the destruction that wasteth at noonday.

A thousand shall fall at thy side, and ten thousand at thy right hand; but it shall not come nigh thee.

Only with thine eyes shalt thou behold and see the reward of the wicked.

Because thou hast made the LORD, which is my refuge, even the most High, thy habitation;

There shall no evil befall thee, neither shall any plague come nigh thy dwelling.

For he shall give his angels charge over thee, to keep thee in all thy ways.

They shall bear thee up in their hands, lest thou dash thy foot against a stone.

Thou shalt tread upon the lion and adder: the young lion and the dragon shalt thou trample under feet.

Because he hath set his love upon me, therefore will I deliver him: I will set him on high, because he hath known my name.

He shall call upon me, and I will answer him: I will be with him in trouble; I will deliver him and honour him.

> *With long life will I satisfy him and shew him my salvation.* (Psalm 91:1–16 KJV)

Amen and amen.

Conclusion

As I come to the end of this book, I can't help but express immense gratitude for those who've walked alongside me. My family, my dear friends, and the timeless wisdom of the Bible have been my guiding lights.

Above all, I'm overwhelmed by thankfulness when I think about the One who has always been there for me, offering unwavering support and boundless love—God the Father, the Son, and the Holy Spirit. In moments of joy and struggles alike, I've felt His comforting presence, His grace, and His constant love.

Lastly, I want to highlight how important it is to include God in your choices. He cares deeply for us, always there, even if we can't see Him (Jeremiah 32:17; Jeremiah 33:3).

Real freedom means understanding what's good and what's harmful. Good things come from the Spirit of Truth, guiding us well. The Spirit of Error leads to things that harm us (1 John 4:6, Galatians 5:19–21).

It's vital to protect our minds from bad influences.

Praying with Scripture for days can change us a lot, connecting us more with what God wants. Letting God guide us brings peace and freedom.

The battle between good and bad thoughts is ongoing. But if we focus on God's Word instead of doubting or being scared, that's real freedom.

Remember, God is always there for you, supporting and helping you. His love can change your life.

Know that God's love never changes, and He can transform your life. Let the changes in you show how amazing and loving He is.

As you finish reading this book, I hope you've felt the depth of His love and the certainty of His guidance. May you also feel sure that God, our Heavenly Father, has your back, walks beside you, guiding your steps and supporting you through everything.

So do your best to do what's right, to stay close to God, and to have faith, love, patience, and gentleness. It is important to stand strong for what you believe in. It is important to fight to maintain your faith.

> Guard what you've been entrusted with. Avoid useless arguments and false teachings that oppose true knowledge. Put in your best effort to win this battle and grasp onto the promise of eternal life. (1 Timothy 6:11, 12 and 20)

> But grow in grace, and in the knowledge of our Lord and Saviour Jesus Christ. To him be glory both now and forever. Amen. (2 Peter 3:18)

> Now may the God of peace make you holy in every way and may your whole spirit and soul and body be kept blameless until our Lord Jesus Christ comes again. God will make this happen, for he who calls you is faithful. (1 Thessalonians 5:23–24)

May the grace of our Lord Jesus Christ be with you all.

Love in Christ,
Reza Mohseni

About the Author

Reza Mohseni, born in Tehran, found his passion for soccer at a young age and moved to the USA alone at seventeen. In 1990, discovering Christ changed his life, prompting him to share this transformative experience with others.

With a profound love for the Lord, Reza reflects Christ's kindness and love in his daily life. His family—four children, their spouses, a stepdaughter, her spouse, and ten grandkids—brings immense joy.

Transitioning from a thirty-year career in banking, Reza responded to a divine calling in 2012, joining the Conquerors League Adult and Youth Soccer and Futsal Ministry in VA, a ministry of Temple Baptist Church. This ministry offers soccer camps, leagues, tournaments, and individual and group training sessions. Our main goal is to encourage faith and build character while guiding people toward God the Father, the Son, and the Holy Spirit through soccer activities. We provide a secure and competitive environment for this purpose.

The Conquerors League Soccer and Futsal Ministry is dedicated to helping young people grow in their spiritual, mental, physical, social, and character development. Our main focus is on the all-around growth of each child, giving importance to participation and enjoyment rather than just winning. We have various programs tailored to different needs, whether for fun, skill improvement, or competitive goals.

Our approach centers around teaching Christlike values such as honesty, responsibility, compassion, and discipline through soccer. Alongside soccer skills, we also emphasize crucial life skills like teamwork, leadership, and communication. Our ultimate goal is to ensure the overall well-being of every player while fostering a strong sense of family and community within our soccer programs.

TBC is a friendly church that focuses on helping people and serving together in the name of Jesus. The pastor's messages every Sunday are enjoyed and loved by the author, who appreciates the pastor's unique way of explaining God's Word so everyone can understand. The pastor's prayers, love, patience, and care are highly valued, and his role has greatly influenced the author's spiritual journey. The pastor is not only committed to preaching God's Word but also serves as a mentor, bringing blessings to the community. The author has been part of TBC for over thirty years and has seen the church grow stronger. The importance of preaching God's Word is emphasized, and the diligent studies of the pastor inspire believers to deepen their relationship with the Lord. The author also praises Temple Baptist School (TBS), which provides a respectful atmosphere for teachers and students. Despite the preference for order, there is a belief in having fun. The author's adult children attended TBS, and now their grandkids are also part of it. If someone is in northern Virginia and searching for a church and school, the author assures that TBC and TBS are ideal choices.

Our soccer and futsal programs have become a tradition for many families, and we hope they earn a special place in yours too.